WHAT WOULD YOU DO:

81 Philosophical Dilemmas for Discussion & Expansion

TAYLOR SAPP

Alphabet PUBLISHING

WHAT WOULD YOU DO?

81 Philosophical Dilemmas for Discussion & Expansion

TAYLOR SAPP

ISBN: 978-1-948492-25-6

Alphabet Publishing
1204 Main Street #172
Branford, CT 06405 USA

info@alphabetpublishingbooks.com

www.alphabetpublishingbooks.com

Discounts on class sets and bulk orders available upon inquiry.

Design by Annabel Brandon

All images from DepositPhotos, UnSplash, and PublicDomainImages.Net, except:
Image of Mars taken by NASA, Public Domain, Image of White House by Andrea Hanks, Public Domain, Image of Statue of Liberty by Derek Jensen, Public Domain, Image of Adolph Hitler, Wikimedia Commons, Public Domain, Image of John F. Kennedy, Official White House Portrait, Public Domain, Trolley Problem adapted from image by McGeddon, CC BY_SA 4.0 from Wikimedia Commons

Author Image by Noah Sapp, age 7, shared by permission

Alphabet Publishing Logo by Joshua Comen.

Country of Manufacture Specified on Last Page

First Printing 2019

Dedication

Special thanks should also be given to friends, family, teachers, and students who helped in the reading and testing of these tricky dilemmas!

Reina Adachi

Mahmoud Al Dweik

Khalaf Alkhalaf

Amal Alghamdi

Abdulelah Aljohan

Afrah Almuraihel

Adnan Alnamer

Saud Alsaiari

Sawsen Alseba

Faisal Almazurui

Asim Alomair

Mezhah Alsharif

Yusuf Bajamil

Stephanie Burns

Yen "Amy" Chen Ko

Wen-Yu "Phoebe" Chang

Katrina Cui

Fahad Dekhayl

Abdullah Dous

Max Forstag

Sandy Fox

Yudai Hasegawa

ELS Portland

David Heinrich

Arisa Isotani

ELS Language Centers

Kengo Ishizuka

Moe Izumi

Ali Jablawi

Hana Jo

Mina Gavell

Caitlin Kaparaz

Peter Lacey

Colleen Loboy

Andrew Lawrence

Boone Nicholson

Catherine Noble

Yui Oya

Chakrit "James" Racchat

Michelle Ridder

Honoka Sato

Yurie Sato

Nana Takizawa

Yu Tzu "Nicole" Wang

Hanqing "Gino" Zhou

My excellent publisher and editor Walton Burns

And of course, my family, Aya, Quinn, Noah, Susan, Parker, James and Leslie

Contents

SITUATIONS FOR YOUNGER LEARNERS

SITUATIONS FOR TEENAGERS AND YOUNG ADULTS

SITUATIONS FOR ADULTS

ADDITIONAL ACTIVITIES FOR EXPANSION

Introduction: How to Use This Collection

This book is a collection of 81 hypothetical situations for students to discuss. Each topic has been designed to be quick to get started with so that no outside resources are required (although the activities can be extended with research later). The goal is to prompt healthy discussion both inside and outside the classroom.

Finding ways to get students talking (in particular ESL students from diverse countries, with different levels of conversational competence) requires a lot of different techniques. While I've found that conversation prompts can be effective, some students need more guidance than others. That's why this collection has been designed to help guide the students through the discussion process, while still being open-ended enough to allow considerable expansion, if desired!

As an educator with more than 15 years of experience, I started creating content because I wanted versatile and adaptable materials. All of my work comes from practical in-class usage. Therefore, this book is designed to be flexible and easy enough to use to fill various gaps in the classroom. The situations can be used as warmers or fillers, as stand-alone activities, or fun ways to introduce a new unit.

Each activity is divided into the following five steps:

a. **The Situation**: A brief description of the hypothetical situation. Some are simpler and more general, while some refer to more specific, even actual historical, events, especially at the higher complexity level.

b. **The Dilemma**: A one-sentence summary of the issues presented in the situation and the choice students must make.

c. **What Would You Do?** A list of potential answers to the dilemma. These are provided to give students some ideas. However, a blank answer is provided at the end of the list to account for the fact that it would be impossible to list all of the potential choices! This is also a good way to foster expansion of the topic.

d. **Variables**: A list of factors that might change the students' answers to the dilemma. I found it particularly important to add this section, as many of the dilemmas are open to deeper discussion when changing certain aspects of the situation such as the setting and context, or the age, or gender of the actors. There are also some fantastical variables to appeal to students' creativity and imagination, such as the difference between being bitten by a zombie or a vampire! You will want to pick and choose appropriate variables for your students, as many of them go beyond the original context. For example, situations for children may ask how the situation would change if it took place at work, or involved a girlfriend or boyfriend.

e. **Expansion Activities for Discussion and Writing**: This section is primarily designed for taking the situations beyond the warmer stage, and make for great homework assignments. Questions here could be answered in writing as essays or journals, given as interviews, or conducted as debates. While certainly usable in the classroom, the goal of this section was, as the title states, to give options to educators looking to spend more time with any of the situations.

In addition, expansion questions and supplements are provided at the back of the book to allow for deeper exploration of the topics.

Each situation is organized by both complexity and category. The complexity levels are:

a. **Simple** - These situations are designed for the *elementary* level. These topics are simple and straightforward enough to be handed by younger children in the classroom. While some of the topics might not be as interesting for older students, they are designed to be simple enough that they could work well as quick warmers for higher-level students. These topics relate to simple issues in familiar contexts such as school or family. A few are fantasy related-issues about concepts like monsters, magic, and ninjas!

b. **Medium** - These topics are designed for *middle-school/junior high* students with some scalability. Many of these topics start to delve into some issues that teenagers deal with, such as dating or drug abuse. However, people of all ages tend to have opinions on these topics.

c. **Advanced** - These topics venture into more mature areas suitable for *high-school* or *adult* students. Topics related to parenting, serious relationship issues, and serious crisis are included here.

Some topics that are especially scalable (like Simple/Medium or Medium) have been marked as such!

In addition, each situation is categorized into one of the following:

- Friends and Family

- School Life

- Love and Relationships

- Daily Life

- Fantasy and Magic

- Technology and the Future

- Language

- Money and Possessions

- Politics

- Ethics

- Explicit: Part of the power of these hypothetical situations is that you never know what students will say and sometimes the most controversial or even taboo subjects generate the most discussion and debate! However, a few of the situations discuss taboo topics in fairly explicit terms. These discussions may not suit every classroom. For that reason, there is an explicit category. Be sure to read these carefully to be sure they are appropriate. You may consider leaving out bits or adapting it slightly to fit your students.

Finally, a list of supplements is provided to allow for more expansion opportunities inside or outside of the classroom. Whether it be debates, interviews, drama scenes, or other types of activities, flexibility is the goal. My hope for this collection is that it can be as easily used for the occasional 5-minute warmer as for the focus of a debate or discussion for an entire semester!

And since we're being hypothetical, why not use the situations at a job interview, speed dating event, or as a fun party game! I guess the key question keeping with theme, since you are reading this is: How would you use it?

Taylor Sapp

PART I:
SITUATIONS FOR YOUNGER LEARNERS

The following are situations designed for younger learners. Many are based in reality, but others involve fantastic or magical scenarios that kids often dream about.

**Friends &
Family**   ·   *A Bad Meal*

The Situation:

You've been invited to have dinner at a
good friend's house with their family. To
your surprise, the meal they have made is so
terrible that you are barely able to finish the
first bite. The family is all looking at you and
asking, "So, how is it?"

The Dilemma:

**WHAT DO YOU DO WHEN
YOU DON'T LIKE SOMEONE'S
COOKING?**

1. What Would You Do? (Explain your reasoning)

a. Return the pet?

b. Keep the pet and convince your sibling to get the shot?

c. Keep the pet but in a different room than your sibling?

d. Exchange the dog for a different pet?

e. _____

2. Variables: How would it change the situation if...

a. the person who allergic to the pet were:

    i. a parent?

    ii. your roommate

    iii. your partner?

    iv. your best friend?

b. you were the one with the pet allergy?

c. you have children and they had the allergy?

d. your sibling had a cat allergy instead?

e. the dog had an allergy to something in your house?

f. _____

3. Expansion Activities for Discussion and Writing:

a. Do you or someone you know have a pet allergy?

    i. If so, how did they deal with it?

b. Do you or anyone you know have another kind of allergy?

c. **Discuss or write** a short response to one of the following:

    i. What are the best ways to deal with pet or other allergies?

    ii. Pets are important to make us happy.

    iii. Pets are a waste of money and time.

**Friends &
Family**

Bad Hygiene

The Situation:

You sit next to your friend at school each day. That means you can also smell them! Your friend has bad hygiene, and doesn't wash or brush their teeth as often as they should. Almost every day they smell bad, and lots of people are talking bad behind their back about it. Your friend doesn't seem to know about the issue!

The Dilemma:

HOW CAN YOU HELP YOUR FRIEND WITH THEIR HYGIENE PROBLEM?

1. What Would You Do? (Explain your reasoning)

a. Tell your friend about the bad smell directly?

b. Tell your friend about the bad smell indirectly by giving them perfume or cologne as a present?

c. Talk to your parents or your friend's parents about the issue?

d. Make up a reason to tell the other kids not to make fun of your friend?

e. Say nothing and ignore it?

f. _____

2. Variables: How would it change the situation if...

a. your friend knows about the smell but doesn't want to do anything about it?

b. instead of your friend, the person with the bad smell is your...

    i. classmate you don't know well?

    ii. sibling?

    iii. girlfriend or boyfriend?

    iv. teacher?

c. instead of a bad *smell*, your friend usually has...

    i. dandruff?

    ii. excessive flatulence?

    iii. clothing that is...
- old and dirty?
- strange?
- too revealing or sexy?

    iv. _____

3. Expansion Activities for Discussion and Writing:

a. Have you ever been in this kind of situation before?

    i.   If so, what did you do?

b. Have your ever been the one with bad hygiene?

    i.   If so, did anyone talk to you about it?

c. Is good *hygiene* important to you?

d. How do you compare to your friends and family?

    i.   Who do you know that's the most/least careful about hygiene?

e. Is good hygiene more important for different ages or genders?

f. **Write a short response**: Look at the following saying: *"Cleanliness is next to godliness"*

    i.   What does this mean?

    ii.   Do you agree or disagree? Why?

Friends & Family   ·   # Don't Bug Me!

The Situation:

You are home alone. A big, scary spider is walking across your floor. Your sibling usually likes to catch spiders and put them outside but they are not home right now.

The Dilemma:

IS IT ALWAYS OK TO KILL INSECTS?

1. What Would You Do? (Explain your reasoning)

   a. Smash the spider with something?

   b. Try to pick up the spider and put it outside?

   c. Try to find someone to help you take care of the spider?

   d. Ignore the spider?

   e. Keep the spider as a pet?

   f. _____

2. Variables: How would it change the situation if...

   a. the spider is...

       i. smaller than your fingernail?

       ii. as big as a tarantula!)

       iii. poisonous?

   b. instead of a spider, the insect is a...

       i. fly?

       ii. bee?

       iii. mosquito?

       iv. cockroach?

       v. _____

   c. instead of an insect, you see a mouse!

   d. _____

3. Expansion Activities for Discussion and Writing:

    a. Have you ever been in this kind of situation before?

        i. If so, what did you do?

    b. Is killing insects ever wrong? Why or why not?

    c. What do you usually do when you see an insect…

        i. In your house or room?

        ii. Outside?

    d. Are some insects more ok to kill than others?

        i. Which insects are you most likely to kill?

        ii. Which insects are you least likely to kill?

    e. Discuss or write a short response to the prompts:

        i. All life on earth has value, including insects.

        ii. Insects don't deserve the same rights as animals.

**Friends &
Family** · *Scary Pet!*

The Situation:

You come home to see that your sibling
has gotten a new pet — a giant snake!
They have also decided to surprise you by
keeping it in your shared bedroom. So you
will be meeting the snake every day! And
right now, it's feeding time for the snake's
favorite food, a live mouse!

The Dilemma:

**HOW DO YOU FEEL ABOUT
SHARING A ROOM WITH A
SCARY PET?**

1. What Would You Do? (Explain your reasoning)

   a. Tell your sibling to get rid of the snake?

   b. Tell your sibling to move the snake?

   c. Ignore the snake but refuse to feed it?

   d. Help feed it?

   e. _____

2. Variables: How would it change the situation if...

   a. the snake was smaller?

   b. the snake only eats dead insects?

   c. instead of your sibling, you are living with your...

       i. school roommate?

       ii. best friend?

       iii. boyfriend or girlfriend?

   d. instead of a snake, the pet your sibling got was a...

       i. tarantula?

       ii. iguana?

       iii. Malagasy hissing cockroach?

   e. _____

3. Expansion Activities for Discussion and Writing:

   a. Have you ever been in this situation before?

       i. If so, what did you do?

   b. Do you or someone you know have an unusual pet?

       i. What is it, and what did you think about it?

   c. What unusual pet (something besides a cat or dog) would you be...

       i. Most interested in having?

       ii. Least interested in having?

   d. **Write/Discuss a short response**: Answer one of the following questions:

       i. Which is the better pet: a cat or dog?

       ii. What is the best _unique_ pet choice?

Friends & Family · *Smile, Please!*

The Situation:

You have a friend with one issue that bothers you and others: They are always way too serious! They almost never smile and always act sad or depressed. Even when you say something nice or give them a present they never smile! When you try to bring it up, your friend just says it's their "natural way." But, as a result, people are starting to staying away from your friend more and more!

The Dilemma:

IS BEING TOO SERIOUS A PROBLEM?

1. What Would You Do? (Explain your reasoning)

a. Have a long, honest talk with your friend?

b. Try to get your friend to go to a psychiatrist or doctor?

c. Find a fun activity to do with your friend?

d. Talk to someone else (parent/teacher/other friend) and try to get them to help you talk to your friend?

e. Say nothing?

f. _____?

2. Variables: How would it change the situation if...

a. your friend is the opposite gender?

b. your friend is the same gender and gay?

c. instead of a friend, the serious person is your family member?

    i. sibling (Does it matter if it's your brother or sister)?

    ii. parent or grandparent?

    iii. other family (Does it matter if it's your uncle, aunt, or cousin)?

d. Instead of a friend, the serious person is your...

    i. classmate, whom you don't know well?

    ii. teacher?

    iii. boss?

e. _____

3. Expansion Activities for Discussion and Writing:

a. Have you ever had friends/family that were too serious in behavior?

    i. If so, what did you do?

b. Have you ever had any friends and family that were too silly and not serious?

    i. If so, what did you do?

    ii. Which is worse: someone who is too serious, or too silly and always joking?

c. **Write a short essay or discuss** whether you agree or disagree with any of the following statements:

    i. People who smile more are happier.

    ii. Smiling at strangers will make you happier.

    iii. People today are pressured to smile too much.

**School Life,
Ethics**

Making Excuses

The Situation:

You stayed up late last night playing video games and forgot to do your homework. Even worse, you overslept and now you know you will be late to class. Your first period class is very difficult and you are in danger of failing. Your teacher is tough and seems especially hard on you. Telling the truth could get you in big trouble, but so could telling a lie!

The Dilemma:

DO YOU MAKE UP EXCUSES FOR BEING LATE AND NOT DOING YOUR HOMEWORK?

1. What Would You Do? (Explain your reasoning)

a. Tell the teacher the truth, that you overslept and didn't do your homework.

b. Go to school and make up an excuse for why you are late but tell the truth about not doing your homework?

c. Go to school and make up an excuse for why you are late and also an excuse for not doing your homework?

d. Pretend to be sick and stay home?

e. _____

2. Variables: How would it change the situation if...

a. the teacher is very kind and understanding?

b. your friend offers to let you copy their homework?

c. you have an important test in your first class?

d. your homework and attendance are perfect so far?

e. _____

3. Expansion Activities for Discussion and Writing:

a. Have you ever been in this situation before?

    i. If so, what did you do? What excuse did you tell?

b. Are you (or were you) usually good about...

    i. Doing your homework?

    ii. Being on time to class?

c. Are there some situations where not doing your homework or being late to school is ok? What are they?

d. **Discuss or write a short response**: A common excuse for not doing homework is: My dog ate my homework.

    i. Try to think of the most creative excuses you can for not doing your homework or being late to school!

**School Life,
Ethics** · *Hard Test*

The Situation:

You are taking a very difficult and important test. Even though you worked very hard, you're not sure you can pass! Next to you, you can see a student who looks to be cheating by secretly copying answers from a small piece of paper!

The Dilemma:

DO YOU STOP THE CHEATER?

1. What Would You Do?

    a. Raise your hand and tell the teacher immediately?

    b. Wait until the test is over and tell the teacher privately?

    c. Talk to the cheater after the test and tell them to be honest with the teacher?

    d. Say nothing?

    e. Copy the cheater's answers and cheat too?

    f. _____

2. Variables: How would it change the situation if...

    a. the cheater is your best friend?

    a. the cheater is your boyfriend or girlfriend?

    b. the cheater is a guy or girl you are attracted to?

    c. the cheater is someone you really hate who often bullies you?

    d. the cheater offers you money not to say anything?

    e. you really hate the teacher?

    f. the person with the highest score on the test will get full scholarship to a good university?

    g. _____

3. Expansion Activities for Discussion and Writing

    a. Have you ever been in this situation before?

        i. If so, what did you do?

    b. Should students be responsible for telling the teacher about cheaters?

        i. Why or why not?

    c. Are there any cases where you think cheating is ok?

    d. Discuss or write a short response:

        i. Cheaters Never Prosper:
- What does this saying mean?
- Do you agree or disagree?

        ii. What are the reasons students cheat?
- Is there ever a good reason to cheat?
- How can teachers or students stop cheaters?

**School
Life**

School Uniforms

The Situation:

Your school is making an important decision about whether or not to require school uniforms. Teachers, parents, and students are all being asked to vote, and the deciding vote has amazingly come down to you!

There are two decisions to make: First, should all students should be required to wear school uniforms? Second, should the men's and women's uniforms should be different? Some people are now strongly arguing that it's sexist to make men and women dress differently, especially to make women wear short skirts, for example!

The Dilemma:

SHOULD STUDENTS WEAR UNIFORMS, AND SHOULD THE UNIFORMS FOR BOYS AND GIRLS BE DIFFERENT?

1. What Would You Do? (Explain your reasoning)

    a. Choose school uniforms that are different for boys and girls.

    b. Choose to have school uniforms that are the same for boys and girls.

    c. Choose not to have school uniforms?

    d. _____

2. Variables: How would it change the situation if...

    a. your friends and family all pressure you to choose...

        i. uniforms that are the same for boys and girls?

        ii. uniforms that are different for boys and girls?

        iii. no uniforms?

    b. the uniforms design is already chosen and you don't like it?

        i. the boys uniform must be blue?

        ii. the girls uniform must be pink with a skirt?

    c. there is a big difference in the income level of the families at the school?

        i. most of the students are rich?

        ii. most of the students are poor?

    d. most of the other schools nearby have uniforms?

    e. almost none of the schools nearby have uniforms?

    f. _____

3. Expansion Activities for Discussion and Writing:

    a. Have you ever worn a uniform in school before?

        i. If so, what did you like/dislike about it?

        ii. If not, would you have liked to wear a uniform?

    b. What are the benefits and drawbacks of wearing uniforms?

        i. Why do you think some schools require uniforms?

        ii. Why do you think some cultures require school uniforms more than others?

    c. **Write, Discuss, or Debate**: Choose the PRO or CON side:

        i. PRO: School uniforms make students more equal.

        ii. CON: School uniforms strip away students' individuality.

School Life

After School, More School!

The Situation:

You are tired after your first long day of high school. After going home for dinner, your parents tell that they've signed you up for a cram school—3 more hours of studying at a special school, every night from 6-9pm to help you get ready for college practicing math, language, and other skills for exams.

You're not happy about this, but your parents warn you that other students are doing this too and if you want to have a good future you need to start doing this for the next 6 years!

The Dilemma:

HOW DO YOU FEEL ABOUT CRAM SCHOOL?

1. What Would You Do? (Explain your reasoning)

a. Agree with your parents and work hard at cram school?

b. Refuse to go?

c. Try to convince your parents to do another type of activity instead?

d. _____

2. Variables: How would it change the situation if...

a. you are in...

   i.   Elementary school

   ii. Junior high

b. the cram school is focused on...

   i.   math?

   ii. writing?

   iii. art or music?

c. all of your friends are also going to the cram school?

d. none of your friends are going to the cram school?

e. _____

3. Expansion Activities for Discussion and Writing:

a. Did you go to a cram school?

   i.   If so, how did you feel about it?

   ii. If not, would you have been willing to go?

b. Cram schools are very popular throughout some parts of the world such as Asia, with many students studying up to 6 days a week until 11pm at night!

   i.   What are the benefits of cram schools?

   ii. What are the drawbacks?

c. In America and most Western countries, cram schools are not common. Why do you think that is?

d. **Discuss or write a short response** to one of the following statements:

   i.   Cram schools are an important part of a child's education.

   ii. The more students study, the more success they will have in life.

   iii. There are more important things for children to do than studying.

**School
Life**

Teacher's Pet

The Situation:

You are taking a very hard class with a strict teacher. Doing well in this class will really help your chances of going to a good university! Only one of the students in the class is doing well, because they are a real teacher's pet. They are always bringing an apple or small gift for the teacher, always raising their hand eagerly, and you've heard them tell this teacher that they are the best teacher!

Everyone else in the class is annoyed at the teacher's pet, who is also your friend. They act the same way with all the teachers. You're trying to consider if you should talk to your friend, or be a teacher's pet too!

The Dilemma:

CAN YOU BE A TEACHER'S PET?

1. What Would You Do? (Explain your reasoning)

    a. Tell your friend to not be so much of a teacher's pet?

    b. Become a teacher's pet too?

    c. Try to convince everyone to be teacher's pets?

    d. Say nothing?

    e. Cheat to do better in class?

    f. _____

2. Variables: How would it change the situation if...

    a. the teacher's pet is...

        i. your best friend?

        ii. your brother or sister?

        iii. someone you really don't like?

        iv. your boyfriend or girlfriend?

        v. a boy or girl you like?

    b. the teacher is...

        i. a young, attractive man or woman?

        ii. very old and mean?

        iii. your parent or relative?

    c. you must get an A in this class to go to college?

    d. _____

3. Expansion Activities for Discussion and Writing:

    a. Have you ever been in this situation before?

        i. Were you or someone you know a teacher's pet?

    b. What are the positives or negatives about being a teacher's pet?

    c. In America, bringing an apple for the teacher is a traditional sign of respect. What do they do in other countries?

    d. Discuss or write a short response to one of the following statements:

        i. Teachers don't get enough respect.

        ii. Teachers have to earn respect from students.

Daily Life, Money & Possessions, Ethics

Homeless Help

The Situation:

Walking down the street, you see a homeless man asking for money. He looks fairly young, like he might be able to work. You have several bills and coins in your pocket.

The Dilemma:

SHOULD YOU GIVE HOMELESS PEOPLE MONEY? HOW MUCH?

1. What Would You Do? (Explain your reasoning)

a. Give him some money?

b. Apologize and tell him you don't have money?

c. Ignore him?

d. Call the police to check if he can be moved?

e. Join him and ask for money also?

f. _____

2. Variables: How would it change the situation if the homeless person is...

a. an old man or woman over 60 years old?

b. a child?

c. a man or woman with a dog?

d. a family?

e. someone missing an arm or leg?

f. looks like they have alcohol or drugs?

g. _____

3. Expansion Activities for Discussion and Writing:

a. Have you ever been in this situation before? If so, what did you do? Did you give something to a homeless person?

b. Do you think its ok for homeless people to ask for money in the street? Is it common in your home city or country?

c. What causes people to become homeless?

d. Which kind of homeless people need the most help?

e. Discuss or write a short response to one of the following:

    i. What are the causes of homelessness?

    ii. What can we do to help homeless people?

Daily Life, Ethics · # Hot Car

The Situation:

Walking down the street on a hot summer day, you see a parked car with a dog sitting in the backseat. The windows are closed and the dog is barking!

The Dilemma:

DO YOU TRY AND HELP THE DOG?

1. What Would You Do? (Explain your reasoning)

   a. Call the police?

   b. Break the car window?

   c. Wait by the car until the owner comes back?

   d. Ignore the dog because it's none of your business?

   e. _____

2. Variables: How would it change the situation if...

   a. it's a cold day?

   b. the car's engine was running?

   c. the dog looked quiet and happy?

   d. the dog was asleep or unconscious?

   e. you saw someone else calling the police?

   f. there was a baby in the car instead?

   g. _____

3. Expansion Activities for Discussion and Writing

   a. Have you ever been in this situation before? If so, what did you do?

   b. Should it be against the law to leave an animal or young child alone in a car? Why or why not?

   c. Are there any situations where people should interfere to help if an owner is being cruel to their dog?

    i. yelling

    ii. beating

    iii. other _____

   d. Discuss or write a short response to one of the following:

    i. Do animals and humans deserve the same rights and protection?

    ii. How should the laws or rules be similar or different to protect babies or children in this type of situation?

**Daily Life,
Money &
Possessions,
Ethics**

Lost Wallet

The Situation:

You're walking down the street alone when
you see something on the ground. Stopping
to pick it up, you notice it's a small wallet.
You look around to see if you can find the
owner, but you don't see anyone nearby.
Inside you find a large amount of money
and an ID card.

The Dilemma:

DO YOU TRY TO RETURN THE WALLET?

1. What Would You Do? (Explain your reasoning)

   a. Take the wallet to the police station?

   b. Try to contact the owner directly?

   c. Keep the wallet?

   d. _____?

2. Variables: How would it change the situation if...

   a. the wallet has less than $10 in it?

   b. over $1,000 in it?

   c. no pictures or ID?

   d. the phone number of the owner?

   e. lots of personal pictures?

   f. nude pictures?

   g. _____

3. Expansion Activities for Discussion and Writing:

   a. Has this ever happened to you before? If so, what happened?

      i. Have you found a wallet?

      ii. Did you lose your wallet?

   b. What do you think is the worst thing to lose in your wallet? What is most irreplaceable?

   c. If you lost your wallet, how likely do you think you'd be to get it back...

      i. In America?

      ii. In another country?

      iii. In a big city? In a small city?

      iv. In a rich neighborhood? In a poor neighborhood?

   d. Research: The Lost Wallet Test has been done around the world. People leave wallets in cities around the world to see how many are returned. Look up some results of this test.

      i. Was it surprising? Do people tend to be honest about returning lost things?

      ii. Try doing your own experiment! Drop a wallet in a public place and watch what people do. Be careful what you leave in your wallet though

Technology & Future ·

Go to Mars

The Situation:

The first ever trip to Mars with humans is about to happen and one of the people chosen to go is — YOU! 100 men, women, and children will be going with scientists to set up a colony, a real living city on Mars. You will be one of the first to truly live on another planet. The catch is the trip will take more than 20 human years each way so most likely you can never come back, although you won't age during the trip because of the way you will travel! You can also give away or sell your chance if you don't want to go, but can you turn down the opportunity?

The Dilemma:

ARE YOU WILLING TO SPEND THE REST OF YOUR LIFE AS A MARTIAN?

1. What Would You Do?

a. Accept the position and leave for Mars forever?

b. Give the chance to someone else you know?

c. Sell the chance to someone else who wants to go?

d. Turn down the opportunity?

e. _____

2. Variables: How would it change the situation if...

a. the 100 people going to Mars are all from...

   i.   your school?

   ii.   your neighborhood?

   iii.   all speak the same language?

   iv.   all speak different languages?

   v.   all are the opposite gender from you?

b. instead of forever, the round-trip will take...

   i.   five years?

   ii.   ten years?

   iii.   twenty years?

c. You are allowed to bring one person with you? Would you choose your...

   i.   mother?

   ii.   father?

   iii.   brother or sister?

   iv.   best friend?

   v.   boyfriend or girlfriend?

   vi.   _____

3. Expansion Activities for Discussion and Writing:

    a. Do you think we will live on other planets in the future?

        i.   How long from now?

        ii.   Would you be willing to live on another planet?

    b. How would life on another planet be different?

        i.   What would be the biggest challenges?

        ii.   Do you think there would be any advantages or benefits?

    c. **Write a short essay or discuss** your answer to agree or disagree with the following statements:

        i.   Humanity should focus its efforts on exploring other worlds that we might inhabit.

        ii.   Humanity should focus on fixing the problems on our planet before looking into space.

Technology & Future, Language · *Information Download*

The Situation:

A new company is selling information in a very special way — downloading it straight into your brain! A new language, social skills, a martial art, it's possible to learn almost anything instantly! You were lucky to be gifted with the very expensive opportunity to choose one type of information to download directly into your mind. So, what do you want to learn?

The Dilemma:

WHAT KIND OF INFORMATION WOULD YOU LIKE TO LEARN INSTANTLY?

1. What Would You Do?

    a. choose to download directly into your brain one of the following:

        i. a new language?

        ii. better social skills?

        iii. a martial arts skill?

        iv. computer or other business skills?

        v. _____

    b. Give or sell the gift coupon to someone else?

    c. _____

2. Variables: How would it change the situation if...

    a. you are trying to get into a great college?

    b. you want to get a great or high-paying job?

    c. the skill or information only lasted 1 week?

    d. you could alter your personality?

    e. you could add, change, or delete memories?

    f. you are very weak and not good at protecting yourself?

    g. _____

3. Expansion Activities for Discussion and Writing:

    a. Do you think downloading information to the brain could ever be possible? Why or why not?

        i. Is it important to study to learn something new on your own? Do you considering downloading information straight to the brain cheating?

    b. **Write a short essay or discuss** your answer to one of the following questions:

        i. The process of studying or working hard to learn something is more important that what you learn.

        ii. Many people study too much when they should be other things that are more important.

Technology & Future ·

Smart Contacts

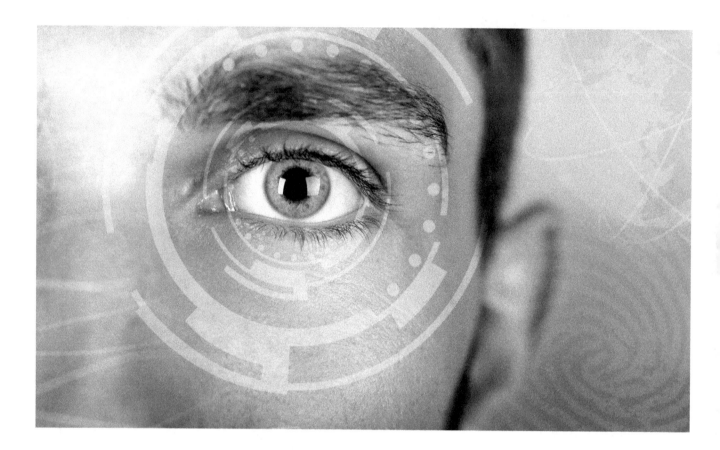

The Situation:

Smart Contacts are the most exciting new technology. These are miniature devices that fit right in your eye like contact lenses! You can use the internet, make calls, take pictures, or watch TV or movies, and no one will know what you're doing!

The Smart Contacts can also be used to monitor your health and location all of the time! Most of your friends have started using these, but you're feeling unsure about the lack of privacy and control!

The Dilemma:

IS IT IMPORTANT TO BE CONNECTED ALL THE TIME?

1. What Would You Do? (Explain your reasoning)

   a. Convince your parents to let you get the Smart Contacts?

   b. Wait until all your friends have the Smart Contacts and see how they're using them?

   c. Forget about the Smart Contacts and avoid using them?

   d. _____

2. Variables: How would it change the situation if...

   a. Smart Contacts are very expensive?

      i. Or free?

   b. Smart Contacts can change your eye color or shape?

   c. Smart Contacts can automatically translate any language?

   d. Smart Contacts can suggest how to respond to any conversation?

   e. Smart Contacts can be tracked by your school/work or your family at all times?

      i. to check your healthy?

      ii. to check your location?

   f. _____?

3. Expansion Activities for Discussion and Writing:

   a. Do you think this technology could be real in the future?

      i. Why or why not?

   b. What other smart technology have you used?

   c. Is there any smart technology that doesn't exist that you'd like to see?

   d. What other features might be useful with Smart Contacts? Write and/or draw a list or picture of useful features!

   e. Debate! Do smartphones make us smarter or dumber?

   f. **Write a short essay or discuss** your answer to agree or disagree with the following statements:

      i. Being connected makes our lives easier.

      ii. We are too dependent on smart technology.

Technology &
Future · *UFO Sighting*

The Situation:

You're driving alone at night on a road deep in the countryside. Suddenly you see a flashing light in the sky. As you watch, it lands in a field near you. You stop your car to check it out and see what clearly looks like an alien spacecraft! A little green person appears in the field, walking towards you!

The Dilemma:

HOW WILL YOU HANDLE FIRST CONTACT WITH ALIENS?

1. What Would You Do? (Explain your reasoning)

a. Approach the alien in peace?

b. Attack the alien?

c. Run back to your car and escape?

d. _____

2. Variables: How would it change the situation if...

a. the alien ship was outside your house?

b. you were with a friend or family member?

c. the alien spoke and asked you to come to its spaceship?

d. the alien had a necklace of human ears around its neck?

e. _____

3. Expansion Activities for Discussion and Writing

a. Do you think this situation could ever be possible?

    i.   Why or why not?

b. Can you think of any TV shows or movies that show aliens visiting Earth?

    i.   Were the aliens friendly or dangerous?

c. Do you believe that aliens exist on other planets?

    i.   If so, do you think aliens have ever come to Earth?

d. More alien questions for **writing and discussion**: If aliens from another planet came to Earth...

    i.   Would they be more likely to be helpful or dangerous?

    ii.   Who should make first contact with them?

    iii.   Is there anything you think they might teach us?

Language— Simple/ Medium

· *Universal Translator*

The Situation:

A new device, the Universal Translator, has been released! It's a small earpiece that can automatically translate any spoken language into your own! As a result, the number of people studying foreign languages is rapidly decreasing. You were hoping to start studying a new language but your friends and family say it's a waste of time because of this new device. They are all telling you the same time could be spent learning something else!

The Dilemma:

CAN TECHNOLOGY REPLACE LANGUAGE STUDY?

1. What Would You Do? (Explain your reasoning)

   a. Use the Universal Translator and forget about studying languages?

   b. Ignore your friends and family and start studying a new language anyways?

   c. Instead of studying a new language, study something else instead!

      i. A musical instrument?

      ii. Ancient history?

      iii. Computer programming?

      iv. _____

   d. _____

2. Variables: How would it change the situation if...

   a. there were no more language classes available so you can only study online or from a book?

   b. the Universal Translator were free for all people?

   c. the Universal Translator were very expensive? Would you buy it if it were...

      i. $10,000?

      ii. $100,000

      iii. $1,000,000?

   d. _____

3. Expansion Activities for Discussion and Writing:

   a. Do you think this situation could ever be possible?

      i. Why or why not?

   b. What are the benefits or disadvantages of a Universal Translator?

   c. Do you think language study will be different in the future? How do you think technology will affect studying languages?

   d. In 10/50/100 years?

   e. **Write about or discuss** the following quote: *"Learning another language is like becoming another person."* —Haruki Marukami, author

      i. What does this quote mean?

      ii. Do you agree or disagree? Why?

**Fantasy &
Magic**   ·   # *Three Wishes*

The Situation:

While looking for something in your grandparents' attic, you find lots of old antiques from their travels. You pick up a small silver oil lamp that looks like it came from *Aladdin* and try to rub the dust off to get a better look.

Suddenly, a genie pops out of the lamp! "Congratulations, you have a pure heart worthy of the magic powers of this lamp! You have 3 wishes to make, anything of your choosing, but there are rules."

You cannot wish for more wishes!

You cannot wish to change people's feelings or hurt anyone (like making someone fall in love with you or wishing someone dead).

You must share two of your wishes! After making your first wish, you must name two other people…

- that will benefit from your wishes!
- and each receive one wish of their own!

Once the three wishes are finished, the genie and the lamp will disappear and find another suitable person!

The Dilemma:

IF YOU HAD ONE WISH, WHAT WOULD YOU WISH FOR? AND WHO WOULD YOU SHARE WISHES WITH?

1. What Would You Do? (Explain your reasoning)

a. Who else would you choose to share your wishes with?

    i.   parents?

    ii.   brother or sister?

    iii.   best friend?

    iv.   boyfriend/girlfriend?

    v.   _____

b. For your three wishes, would you wish for?

    i.   money?

    ii.   academic or work success?

    iii.   good health?

    iv.   beauty?

    v.   _____

2. Variables: How would it change the situation if...

a. you can make all three wishes yourself…

    i.   but it must be in one day?

    ii.   you have as much time as you want?

b. you are allowed to wish to control people's feelings? Would you make someone…

    i.   fall in love with you?

    ii.   dislike another person or thing?

    iii.   _____

c. after you make the three wishes, you will become the next genie?

d. your grandparents ask who you are talking to upstairs? Will you tell them the truth?

e.   _____

3. Expansion Activities for Discussion and Writing:

a. Have you read any books or seen any movies about genies? What did the people wish for in those stories?

b. If you were a genie, how would you choose someone worthy to grant wishes to?

c. If you were a genie, would you change any of the rules in this situation?

d. Write about or discuss one of the following:

    i. What is the difference between hope and wish? How do we use them differently in our lives?

    ii. The ability to wish separates us from animals in what ways?

    iii. Wish in one hand, spit in the other; see which fills up first!

Fantasy & Magic · *Ghost in Your Room!*

The Situation:

You feel lucky to move into a new house with your family and to have your own private bedroom and bathroom! You are so happy until you start to hear strange noises as night! You also start to hear a woman's voice, and even when you are alone you feel like there is someone in the room with you! One day, when looking in the mirror, you even see what looks like a woman's face, but when you turn around, there's no one there, only a message on your mirror that says "GET OUT!" You tell your family but they think you are just watching too many scary movies!

The Dilemma:

HOW CAN YOU DEAL WITH A GHOST IN YOUR ROOM?

1. What Would You Do? (Explain your reasoning)

a. Try to communicate with the ghost, hoping that it's peaceful?

b. Get your friend or family to stay in the room to check if they can see the ghost?

c. Hire someone to get rid of the ghost?

d. Ignore the idea of a ghost because you don't believe in them?

e. Decide it must be a joke?

f. _____

2. Variables: How would it change the situation if...

a. the ghost is peaceful and wants to be friends?

    i. the ghost wants to be your new best friend?

    ii. the ghost wants to be your romantic partner?

b. the ghost is evil and says it will kill you if you don't leave?

c. instead of your own room, the ghost is...

    i. in your classroom at school?

    ii. at your office or part-time job?

    iii. in your new apartment where you're living alone?

d. _____?

3. Expansion Activities for Discussion and Writing:

a. Do you think a situation like this could ever be possible?

    i. Have you or anyone you know had a ghost in their house or apartment before?

b. Do you believe in ghosts? Why or why not?

    i. If you believe in ghosts, do you believe they are usually good or evil? Why?

c. **Research**: Talk to a friend or family about their own experience with a ghost.

    i. Where did they see it?

    ii. When did it happen?

    iii. What happened?

    iv. Was the ghost friendly or dangerous?

    v. Do you believe this ghost was real?

d. **Write a short essay or discuss** your answer to one of the following statements:

    i. Ghosts are superstition and not real.

    ii. Ghosts are real and tend to be...(choose good/evil/both!)

Fantasy & Magic · *Look Who's Speaking!*

The Situation:

You've just gotten your first pet and you're very excited! Your new macaw is able to copy human speech, so you're excited to try talking to him! When you say, "Hello," he says, "Hello," right back! Anything you say, he can repeat! But then he starts saying a lot more. He tells you about where he's from, what he likes to eat, and his favorite movies. He can even talk about religion and politics.

This is no normal bird…This is a very special, one-of-a-kind pet!

The Dilemma:

WHAT SHOULD YOU DO WITH YOUR SPECIAL PET?

1. What Would You Do? (Explain your reasoning)

    a. Show your family and friends?

    b. Post videos online of your bird's conversations?

    c. Try to sell your bird and get rich?

    d. Keep your macaw's talking a secret?

    e. _____

2. Variables: How would it change the situation if...

    a. instead of a macaw, your talking pet is a...

        i. dog?

        ii. cat?

        iii. horse?

        iv. cockroach?

        v. other _____

    b. you were offered 1 million dollars for your macaw? Would you sell him for less? If so, how much?

    c. your macaw became a famous actor?

        i. What other kinds of jobs could your macaw do? Would you let him?

3. Expansion Activities for Discussion and Writing

    a. Do you think animals will be able to talk to humans in the future?

        i. What kind of animals are most able to talk to humans?

    b. If animals could really talk, how would that change our lives?

        i. For example, would you be willing to eat an animal such as a chicken if it could talk to you?

    c. Write a short essay or discuss your answer to agree or disagree with the following statements:

        i. Sometimes your pet can understand you better than humans.

        ii. Pets are sometimes better than friends.

Fantasy & Magic · *Magic Wand*

The Situation:

You are walking down the street one day when you come across a man dressed as a wizard. When he sees you, his eyes light up: "It's you! The chosen one! My time is near an end and I must pass on my wand before I go!" He offers you his wand, which he says is magic! "Picture anything, wave your hand, say the magic words, and it will come true! Now come with me: the time to fight the evil dragon is now. It will be a dangerous fight but the world will surely fail without your help!"

The Dilemma:

DO YOU WANT TO BE A WIZARD WITH THE POWER TO SAVE THE WORLD?

1. What Would You Do? (Explain your reasoning)

a. Accept the offer to become a wizard and leave with him immediately?

b. Accept the offer but try to ask the wizard for more time?

c. Reject the wizard's offer?

d. Try to recommend someone else to the wizard?

e. _____

2. Variables: How would it change the situation if...

a. you know you can save the world, but you will also die?

b. the wizard asks you to begin years of magic school training?

c. the wizard asks you to recommend someone else?

d. _____

3. Expansion Activities for Discussion and Writing

a. Do you think magic is real? Why or why not?

b. What do you know about wizards or witches?

    i. Have you ever watched any movies or TV shows about magic? If so, how did they depict magic?

c. What do you think about stage magicians? Would you want to do this job?

    i. Why do you think people enjoy magicians so much, especially since we know stage magic isn't real?

d. **Write about or discuss** your answer to the following quote:

    i. *"Magic's just science that we don't understand yet."*— Attributed to Arthur C. Clarke, science fiction writer

**Fantasy &
Magic**   · *Ninja Assassin*

The Situation:

Bad news! You've made the wrong person angry, and they've hired a ninja assassin to kill you! You receive a mysterious note saying that you have three days to say your goodbyes, and then the ninja is coming for you!

The Dilemma:

HOW CAN YOU SURVIVE THE UNKNOWN ATTACK OF A NINJA ASSASSIN?

1. What Would You Do? (Explain your reasoning)

a. Run away to another city or country?

b. Buy a weapon and fight the ninja?

c. Accept your fate and enjoy your last three days?

d. Assume it's a joke and do nothing?

e. _____

2. Variables: How would it change the situation if...

a. you know that it is true?

b. instead of you, the ninja will kill a friend or family member?

c. You have advanced ninja training yourself?

d. Instead of a ninja, a mugger on the street pulls a gun and says they will kill you if you don't give all your money?

e. _____

3. Expansion Activities for Discussion and Writing

a. Do you think ninjas or other types of assassins are real? Why or why not?

b. What do you know about ninjas?

    i. Have you ever watched any movies or TV shows about ninjas? If so, what did you learn about them?

    ii. Have you watched any other assassin or hitmen on TV/Movies? If so, what did you learn about them?

c. What do you think about a ninja or other type of assassin job?

    i. Could you ever do it?

    ii. What if you only killed dangerous or bad people?

d. **Write about or discuss** one of the questions below related to the following expression: An eye for an eye

    i. What does this expression mean?

    ii. Do you agree or disagree? Why?

    iii. Is it ok to kill a killer? Why or why not?

**Fantasy &
Magic** · *Superhero*

The Situation:

One day when you are walking alone,
you find a strange ring on the ground
with an S written on it. Trying it on, you
find something amazing —it gives you
superpowers! You can lift anything, run
faster than a car, and even fly! In addition, as
long as you're wearing this ring, nothing can
hurt you!

The Dilemma:

HOW DO YOU USE YOUR NEW POWERS?

1. What Would You Do? (Explain your reasoning)

a. Use the ring to start fighting crime?

b. Become the greatest athlete on earth?

c. Steal all the money you want?

d. Travel around the world for free?

e. _____

2. Variables: How would it change the situation if...

a. your ONLY power were...

    i. flying?

    ii. super strength?

    iii. superspeed?

    iv. X-ray vision?

    v. mind control?

b. you can only keep the ring for one week? Then you must pass it to someone else. Who would you give it to?

c. Every day you wear the ring, you lose one year of your lifespan?

d. _____

3. Expansion Activities for Discussion and Writing:

a. Do you think this situation could ever be possible? Why or why not?

b. Who's your favorite superhero from movies, books, or TV?

c. If you could choose only one superpower, which would you choose?

    i. flying

    ii. super strength

    iii. superspeed

    iv. other _____

d. As the world's only superhero, you can only stop one crime at a time. There are many crimes you won't be able to stop! How can you decide which crimes to stop?

e. **Write about or discuss** the questions below about the following expression: With great power comes great responsibility.

    i. What does this expression mean?

    ii. Do you agree or disagree? Why?

**Money &
Possessions** · *Volcano Eruption*

The Situation:

Bad news! You happen to live a little too close to a volcano that is about to erupt! There are loud sirens and warnings telling you to escape from your house right now! You're not supposed to bring anything, but if you act quickly, you might be able to take something important. However, if you are too slow, it could cost you your life!

The Dilemma:

DO YOU TRY TO SAVE SOMETHING, AND IF SO, WHAT?

1. What Would You Do? You can only grab one thing. What do you grab? (Explain your reasoning)

a. Smartphone?

b. Laptop?

c. Personal letter or pictures?

d. Favorite book?

e. Take nothing and escape with your life?

f. _____

2. Variables: How would it change the situation if...

a. you could take two items?

b. you had a bicycle with two seats? Who would you most want to come with you?

c. you were in a wheelchair and couldn't move easily?

d. you had space in your car for only four people. Who would you take with you?
- parents?
- brother or sister?
- best friend?
- grandmother or grandfather?
- your children?
- a stranger with a baby?
- boyfriend/girlfriend?
- dog or cat?

    i. What if you had to leave one of those people behind?

    ii. If you have to leave two of those people behind?

e. _____

3. Expansion Activities for Discussion and Writing:

a. How realistic is this situation? Why or why not?

b. This is an example of a life-and-death situation. How well do you think in these kinds of situations?

    i. Do you think you could be calm?

    ii. Who do you think would be calmest among your family and friends?

c. If your home was about to be destroyed, what would be the most difficult thing to replace?

d. **Write about or discuss** one of the following:

    i. Things can be replaced, but people can't.

    ii. Some things are priceless and can't be replaced.

    iii. Family members are more important than friends.

**Fantasy &
Magic**   · *Zombie Bite*

The Situation:

You're walking home late at night in the dark alone. Suddenly, a strange looking figure approaches you. It has a terrible smell. Without warning, it bites you right on the hand! You pull away and as you do, you can see that it looks like a zombie!

Shocked, you run away leaving the zombie walking slowly towards you in the distance! You check your hand and see a small but very clear bite mark.

The Dilemma:

HOW DO YOU DEAL WITH A ZOMBIE BITE?

1. What Would You Do? (Explain your reasoning)

   a. Go the hospital to have them look at the bite?

   b. Go to the police and report a zombie on the loose?

   c. Assume it's just a crazy person and not worry about it?

   d. Begin to plan for the zombie life?

   e. Cut off your hand to avoid becoming a zombie?

   f. _____

2. Variables: How would it change the situation if...

   a. you could tell it's someone in a zombie costume?

   b. you could tell it's a real zombie?

   c. the zombie was a friend or member of the family member?

   d. a vampire bit you instead?

   e. _____

3. Expansion Activities for Discussion and Writing:

   a. Do you think this situation could ever be possible? Why or why not?

   b. Can you think of any TV shows or movies where people were bitten by zombies? What did the characters do?

   c. If zombies attacked your school right now, what would you do?

   d. More Zombie Talk for writing and discussion:

      i. How would you react in a zombie *apocalypse* where all the people in the world were turned into zombies? Do you think you would be a good survivor?

      ii. What's the best way to survive a zombie apocalypse? Make a list or write about:
- safe places
- necessary supplies
- useful skills

PART II

SITUATIONS FOR TEENAGERS AND YOUNG ADULTS

This section contains situations that are designed for teenagers or young adults. These topics are more mature and complicated than those in the simple section. For example, this section adds a Romance and Relationships category, one that is more appropriate for teenage or older learners.

Drug Users

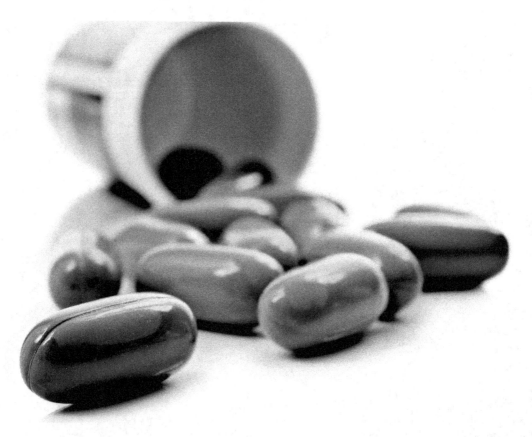

The Situation:

Your best friend has been acting strange lately. Sometimes, their energy seems too high or too low. Your friend's grades at school are getting worse as well. One day, when you are at their house watching a movie alone, you find some mysterious pills. When you ask your friend if they're illegal drugs, your friend tries to change the topic and asks you not to say anything to anyone about it!

The Dilemma:

WHAT DO YOU DO ABOUT YOUR FRIEND'S DRUG PROBLEM?

1. What Would You Do? (Explain your reasoning)

a. Call the police?

b. Tell your friend's parents or teachers about the drugs?

c. Tell your friend to stop using the pills or you will tell someone?

d. Ask your friend to share the drugs?

e. Say nothing and ignore it?

f. _____

2. Variables: How would it change the situation if...

a. the drug is a legal medication but you think your friend is using too much?

b. if you know that the drug is...

   i. marijuana?

   ii. LSD or ecstasy?

   iii. heroin?

   iv. _____

c. you are with three or more friends and they are all using drugs together?

   i. if they ask you to use too?

   ii. if they threaten to hurt you if you say anything?

d. _____

3. Expansion Activities for Discussion and Writing:

a. Have you ever been in this situation before? If so, what did you do?

b. Have you seen this type of situation in a movie, on TV, or in books?

c. Is it ok to use drugs in some situations?

d. Which drugs have you used or are willing to try?

e. Which would you never use?

f. **Discuss or write a short response**: Look at the following saying: *"Drugs take you to hell, disguised as heaven."* — Attributed to Donald Lynn Frost, poet

   i. What does this mean?

   ii. Do you agree or disagree? Why?

Friends & Family · *Touchy Feely*

The Situation:

You have a great friend who is the same gender as you. They have one little habit that annoys you: touching. Your friend always likes to stand too close when talking and touches you on the arm or shoulder a lot. They always want to hug many times when you meet. A little bit of contact might be ok, but they're always so close! You know your other friends feel the same way as you, and they've asked you to say something about this too!

The Dilemma:

CAN YOU STOP YOUR FRIEND FROM TOUCHING SO MUCH?

1. What Would You Do? (Explain your reasoning)

a. Tell your friend the truth?

b. Say nothing but show with your actions that they touch too much?

c. Try hugging and touching your friend too much so they get the point?

d. Talk to someone else (parent/teacher/other friend) and try to get them to help you talk to your friend?

e. Say nothing?

f. _____ ?

2. Variables: How would it change the situation if...

a. your friend is the opposite gender?

b. your friend is the same gender and gay?

c. instead of a friend, they are a member of your family?

  i. brother or sister

  ii. parent or grandparent

  iii. aunt or uncle

  iv. a cousin

  v. other family?

d. it's an adult that likes touching too much?

  i. a friend's parent

  ii. teacher

  iii. boss

e. _____

3. Expansion Activities for Discussion and Writing:

a. Have you ever been in a situation like this before? If so, what did you do?

b. How often do you touch your friends?

  i. Are you ok with hugging friends of the opposite gender? Why or why not?

c. Which is worse: someone who touches too much or someone who stands too close when they talk? Why?

d. **Discuss or write** a short essay agreeing or disagreeing with one of the following opinions:

  i. Cultures where people touch more are closer and friendlier.

  ii. Cultures where people touch less are more respectful.

Friends & Family · # *Waiting for a Friend*

The Situation:

One of your best friends is always late to everything such as going out to restaurants or meeting for shopping. They always miss the train or bus! Right now, you are waiting for them outside a movie theater and the movie is about to start. Your friend isn't answering their phone (as usual!) Your friend always makes you wait and you are getting tired of getting patient!

The Dilemma:

SHOULD YOU BE PATIENT FOR PEOPLE WHO ARE ALWAYS LATE?

1. What Would You Do? (Explain your reasoning)

    a. Keep waiting patiently outside and hope your friend comes soon?

    b. Keep waiting outside but get angry at your friend when they come?

    c. Go inside and get a seat and hope they come?

    d. Leave and text your friend to let them know?

    e. Leave without telling your friend?

    f. Say nothing, but plan on getting revenge later!

    g. _____

2. Variables: How would it change the situation if the person who is always late was...

    a. a member of your family?

        i.   brother/sister

        ii.   mother/father

        iii.   grandparent

    b. your boyfriend or girlfriend?

    c. a boy/girl you like and hope will be your girlfriend/boyfriend?

    d. your boss?

    e. _____

3. Expansion Activities for Discussion and Writing:

    a. Have you (or someone you know) ever been in a situation like this before? If so, did you complain to your friend?

    b. Have your friends ever complained about you being late?

    c. Compared to your friends/family, are you usually early, late, or have the same timing?

    d. **Write a short essay or discuss** whether you agree or disagree with one of the following opinions:

        i.   Being late shows disrespect and that you think you're better than other people.

        ii.   People worry too much about being on time.

Love & Relationships · *Online Dating*

The Situation:

You're lonely, so you start using a dating app online. You meet a really nice person that you enjoy communicating with, and the pictures on their profile are very attractive! You decide to meet for dinner. You're shocked to find the person looks totally different than they did in the pictures. They used a picture of a different person online that was much more attractive. Although the person seems nice, they do not look attractive to you in real life or like the person in the pictures at all!

The Dilemma:

WILL YOU DATE SOMEONE YOU LIKE BUT DON'T THINK IS ATTRACTIVE?

1. What Would You Do? (Explain your reasoning)

a. Comment on how different the person looks but stay for dinner?

b. Get angry and leave?

c. Ignore the person's looks but never meet them again after dinner?

d. Ignore the person's looks and just connect with their personality?

e. _____?

2. Variables: How would it change the situation if your date...

a. is overweight or too thin (anorexic)?

b. is much older or younger than expected?

c. is bald?

d. has lots of visible tattoos or piercings?

e. is much more attractive than the pictures?

f. tells you that they...

    i. have children?

    ii. are divorced?

    iii. are unhappily married and want to have an affair?

g. _____

3. Expansion Activities for Discussion and Writing:

a. Have you ever been in a situation like this before? If so, what did you do?

b. What are your biggest **turn-offs** in dating?

    i. in appearance (size, facial features, muscle, etc.)

    ii. in personality (mean, serious, indecisive, etc.)

    iii. Other _____

c. What are your biggest **turn-ons** in dating?

    i. in appearance (size, facial features, muscle, etc.)

    ii. in personality (kind, funny, decisive, etc.)

    iii. Other _____

d. **Write a short essay or discuss** whether you agree or disagree with one of the following:

    i. Beauty is on the inside.

    ii. Beauty is the most important factor in starting a new relationship.

Friends & Family
Explicit

Public Display of Affection

The Situation:

You're standing in an elevator alone when a young couple walks in. They are holding hands and begin making lots of public displays of affection (PDA). They start hugging and kissing and making lots of noise!

The Dilemma:

ARE YOU OKAY WITH PDA?

1. What Would You Do? (Explain your reasoning)

a. Ignore the couple?

b. Make a sound or grunt of disapproval, but not say anything?

c. Say something to the couple about how their behavior is inappropriate?

d. Say nothing, but take a picture?

e. _____?

2. Variables: How would it change the situation if...

a. the couple are over 70 years old?

b. the couple are under 18 years old?)

c. the man looks older (40 or over) and the girl much younger (under 20)?

d. the woman looks older (40 or over) and the boy much younger (under 20)?

e. you are with your girlfriend/boyfriend?

f. the couple starts taking off their clothes?

g. _____

3. Expansion Activities for Discussion and Writing:

a. Have you ever been in a situation like this before?

    i. If so, what did you do?

b. When and where is PDA appropriate? (Elevators, parks, movie theaters, etc.)

c. How much PDA is appropriate? (hugging, kissing, French kissing, etc.)?

d. **Write a short essay or discuss** whether you agree or disagree with one of the following:

    i. If you love someone, you should make your love public.

    ii. PDA is very disrespectful to those around you.

Friends & Family

Explicit

· # Teenage Love

The Situation:

You have a very young teenager, 12 years old, who has just started dating. They tell you that they have found a special someone and that they are very happy!

Now they are asking you lots of questions about how to have a relationship, and how they can initiate their first kiss! You're a little worried they might be too young and what it might lead to next!

The Dilemma:

HOW YOUNG IS TOO YOUNG FOR ROMANCE?

1. What Would You Do? (Explain your reasoning)

    a. Give them advice on the first kiss?

    b. Try to discourage them from being physical?

    c. Tell them they are too young to have a romantic relationship?

    d. _____

2. Variables: How would it change the situation if...

    a. your child is a boy or girl?

    b. their age is older or younger than 12?

    c. they ask you to have one of the following dates with their partner...

        i. see a romantic movie at the cinema?

        ii. take a dance class together?

        iii. spend the night together?

    d. _____

3. Expansion Activities for Discussion and Writing:

    a. What do you think is the right age to have a first love? Why do you think so?

    b. How old were you when you had your first romantic partner? Do you think you were mature and responsible at that age?

    c. Dating: What do you think are good dates that a romantic couple can have at age...

        i. 12?

        ii. 15?

        iii. 18?

    d. Is having only one romantic partner in their lifetime a good or bad thing? Why?

    e. **Discuss or write** a short response to one of the following statements:

        i. Young love can teach children about life.

        ii. Young teenagers (12-15) aren't mature enough to have a romantic relationship.

        iii. Children need to have lots of romantic experiences to learn about life.

        iv. Heartbreak is an important experience.

Friends & Family

Explicit

Non-Binary Dating

The Situation:

You've started dating a very wonderful person. The last two weeks you've spent with them have been amazing and you think you may be in love.

One day, when doing a special activity together, you are each asked to fill out some forms. Where it says "gender", your new partner writes an X. When you ask them about it, they tell you they are transgender and have changed from the gender they were born with. Also, your partner doesn't want to be called "he" or "she" but "them" instead. You really like this person, but are a little concerned and also wonder why they didn't tell you about this before. They tell

you they were worried you would break up with them if you knew the truth about their gender…

The Dilemma:

CAN YOU DATE A TRANSGENDER PERSON?

1. What Would You Do? (Explain your reasoning)

a. Continue to date the person and accept their transgender identity?

b. Continue to date the person but try to get them to choose a gender identity?

c. Break up with this person and be honest about the reason?

d. Break up with this person but make an excuse?

e. Ask your friends/family and follow their advice?

f. _____

2. Variables: How would it change the situation if...

a. your parents/friends insist you break up with them?

b. your new partner...

    i. was born with a female body but lives as a male?

    ii. was born with a male body but lives as a female?

    iii. is planning to have surgery to change their body to match their chosen gender (pre-op)?

    iv. has already had this surgery (post-op)?

    v. is non-binary, and doesn't think of themselves as having any gender?

c. What other surprises from a romantic partner that you've been seeing for two weeks could change your willingness to keep dating them?

    i. income (they are very rich or poor)?

    ii. youth (They are under 18-20?)

    iii. They are already:
- married?
- have children?

    iv. _____

3. Expansion Activities for Discussion and Writing:

a. If you discovered a surprise about your partner after dating for 2 weeks…

   i. What would make you most likely to stop dating them?

   ii. Would anything make you more likely to keep dating them?

b. **Interview**: Ask your family or friends the following and write down their answers.

   i. Would you be willing to date a transgender person? Why or why not?

   ii. What other situations would make you more or less likely to date a person?

c. **Write about or discuss the following**: Love is about more than gender.

   i. What does this mean?

   ii. Do you agree or disagree?

**School
Life**

· *Close Talker*

The Situation:

A new student at your school is a close talker—they always stand way too close when talking to you or anyone else. This makes people feel very uncomfortable. For some reason, your friends are looking to you to say something.

The new student looks very sad and lonely, and when you try to talk to them, they always come up very close too quickly. You're worried saying something might hurt their feelings, but maybe it needs to be done?

The Dilemma:

WHAT DO YOU DO ABOUT A CLOSE TALKER?

1. What Would You Do? (Explain your reasoning)

a. Tell the closer talker honestly and directly?

b. Tell the close talker indirectly and be very sensitive about their feelings?

c. Try to get someone else to talk to the close talker…

   i.   A teacher?

   ii. One of your friends?

d. Say nothing and ignore it?

e. _____

2. Variables: How would it change the situation if…

a. the close talker was autistic?

b. the close talker also…

   i.   had body odor?

   ii.   had bad breath?

   iii. had a lazy eye?

c. the close talker was a very attractive boy or girl you'd like to date?

d. the close talker moved to your school because they lost a family member recently?

e. _____

3. Expansion Activities for Discussion and Writing:

a. Have you ever been in this situation before? If so, what did you do?

b. Do you have a personal *space bubble*?

   i.   How much space do you need between you and other people?

   ii. Is it different for friends, family, or strangers?

c. **Research and Write** a short response:

   i.   Is the amount of personal space needed different in other cultures or between people of different ages? Why do you think this is?

**Daily
Life** · *Bad Service*

The Situation:

You are at a nice restaurant and the service is unfortunately not very good. The waiter has been very slow and made more than one mistake. Even worse, he has been rude and unfriendly. He tells you that he's in a bad mood due to his recent divorce, which seems like too much personal information! At the end of the meal, it's time to pay and add the customary tip, which is 20% in America, but you feel like this waiter doesn't deserve it. However, one of your friends insists on paying the tip because it would be "rude not to" and because waiters rely on tips for their salary.

The Dilemma:

SHOULD YOU TIP EVEN WHEN THERE'S BAD SERVICE?

1. What Would You Do? (Explain your reasoning)

   a. Tip the waiter 20%?

   b. Tip the waiter less than 20%?

   c. Not tip the waiter at all?

   d. Talk to the manager about the bad service?

   e. _____

2. Variables: How would it change the situation if...

   a. the waiter is...

      i. under 20 years old?)

      ii. over 70 years old?

      iii. very attractive?

   b. you are paying for you and your friends?

   c. one of your friends is paying for everyone?

   d. the restaurant is...

      i. very fancy and expensive?

      ii. cheap and casual?

   e. _____

3. Expansion Activities for Discussion and Writing:

   a. Have you (or someone you know) ever been in a situation like this before? If so, did they say anything?

   b. What is the difference between good and bad service at a restaurant? What are the reasonable expectations for staff?

   c. What do you think about the concept of tipping at American restaurants and other businesses?

      i. What are the benefits?

      ii. What are the drawbacks?

   a. **Write a short essay or discuss** whether you agree or disagree with the following statements:

      i. Tipping encourages workers to provide better service.

      ii. Tipping is unfairly forcing the customer to pay more.

**Daily
Life**   · *Hug Me!*

The Situation:

You walking down the street by yourself, feeling a bit lonely, when you something very interesting: a person standing and holding a large sign that says "Free Hugs!" This person looks even lonelier and sadder than you!

The Dilemma:

DO YOU HUG A TOTAL STRANGER?

1. What Would You Do? (Explain your reasoning)

    a. Hug them?

    b. Ignore them?

    c. Tell them, "No, thank you"?

    d. _____?

2. Variables: How would it change the situation if the hugger is...

    a. a man or a woman?

    b. under 15 or over 60 years old?

    c. very dirty?

    d. very attractive or ugly?

    e. very happy or sad?

    f. _____

3. Expansion Activities for Discussion and Writing:

    a. Have you ever been in this situation before?

        i. If so, what did you do? Did you hug someone who needed it?

    b. Research a **cuddle group** or **cuddle party.**

        i. What is it?

        ii. Would you ever join one? Would you ever pay to go to one? Why or why not?

        iii. Would you like to be a certified cuddler?

    c. **Research and Write**: Make a sign that says "Free Hugs" and go to a public place:

        i. How many hugs did you get?

        ii. How did you feel about the experience?

    d. **Write or discuss** a short response to one of the following statements:

        i. It is necessary for happiness to have someone you can hug every day.

        ii. Cultures or people that hug more are happier.

Money & Possessions · *Left Laptop*

The Situation:

You are working quietly and peacefully on your laptop in a small café while enjoying your coffee or tea. But then one of the downsides of enjoying your delicious drink strikes: You have to go to the bathroom! You are worried about your laptop and not sure what to do with it: Should you put it your backpack and take it to the restroom? Should you leave it? Should you ask someone to watch it? You're especially scared because one of your friends had their laptop stolen recently!

The Dilemma:

SHOULD YOU ALWAYS TAKE YOUR LAPTOP OR VALUABLES TO THE RESTROOM AT A PUBLIC PLACE?

1. What Would You Do? (Explain your reasoning)

a. Leave the laptop and use the restroom?

b. Ask someone to watch your laptop while you use the restroom?

c. Put it in your bag and take it to the bathroom?

d. _____?

2. Variables: How would it change the situation if the café was...

a. empty?

b. full?

c. in a rich part of town?

d. in an area known for crime?

e. in your home city/country?

f. in another city/country?

g. _____

3. Expansion Activities for Discussion and Writing:

a. Have you ever been in this situation before? If so, what did you do?

b. Would you be more or less likely to leave other items such as your jacket or bag while you went to the restroom?

   i.   Would you trust asking a stranger to watch your items?

c. **Discuss or write a short response** to one of the following statements about *theft* (the stealing of personal belongings):

   i.   All thieves should go to jail.

   ii. Thieves should go to jail only if…

**Daily
Life**   · *Loud Neighbor*

The Situation:

You live on the second floor of an apartment building. The person in the apartment directly below you often plays loud, thumping music, sometimes until 1:00 a.m. or later! You've already asked the person to turn down the music once, but he was a huge, intimidating guy who said the music was important for his job and threatened you if you bother him again! You're scared to ask him again but you're losing sleep!

The Dilemma:

**HOW CAN YOU SILENCE A
NOISY NEIGHBOR?**

1. What Would You Do? (Explain your reasoning)

   a. Go to ask your neighbor again nicely?

   b. Talk to some other neighbors and see if you can talk to him together?

   c. Call the landlord?

   d. Call the police?

   e. Say nothing?

   f. Say nothing, but plan on getting revenge later!

   g. _____

2. Variables: How would it change the situation if the loud neighbor was...

   a. an old man with bad hearing watching TV?

   b. a very attractive man or woman that you'd like to date?

   c. a family with a crying baby?

   d. someone with a loud dog that's always barking?

   e. your landlord?

   f. your best friend?

   g. your brother or sister?

   h. _____

3. Expansion Activities for Discussion and Writing:

   a. Have you (or someone you know) ever been in a situation like this before? If so, did they say anything?

   b. What times are ok or not ok for playing loud music or making other noises?

   c. Which types of noises from neighbors bother you the most?

       i. Loud music?

       ii. Dogs or animals?

       iii. Crying babies?

       iv. Other _____

d. Compared to your friends/family, are you usually…

    i.   On time?

    ii.   Late?

    iii.   About the same as your friends or family?

e. **Write a short essay or discuss** whether you agree or disagree with the following adaptations of famous sayings:

    i.   Don't throw stones at your neighbors if your own windows are glass.

    ii.   If you injure your neighbor, better not do it by halves.

    iii.   We make our friends; we make our enemies; but God makes our next-door neighbor.

**Daily
Life**

· *No Shoes, No Service!*

The Situation:

You decide to move into a new apartment with two new roommates. Inside the door you find a sign saying that you must remove your shoes. In your house growing up you never did this and you find it annoying. The apartment floor is wood and both cold and slippery, but at least the place is clean! Both the apartment and the roommates seem perfect except for this little detail.

The Dilemma:

DO YOU MIND TAKING OFF YOUR SHOES INSIDE YOUR HOME?

1. What Would You Do? (Explain your reasoning)

   a. Agree to take off your shoes and move in!

   b. Agree to take off your shoes and move in, but sometimes still wear them if no one is home!

   c. Move in but try to change their minds?

   d. Find another apartment?

   e. _____

2. Variables: How would it change the situation if...

   a. your roommates have a dog or cat?

   b. there are young children living in the house?

   c. the apartment floor is dirty?

   d. the roommates are your…

       i. siblings?

       ii. best friends?

   e. _____

3. Expansion Activities for Discussion and Writing:

   a. Have you ever been asked to take off your shoes in home? Or have you ever asked others to take their shoes off?

   b. Did you take your shoes off at your home growing up? Did you agree or disagree with this?

   c. Is there anything you did or can do at home to make it more safe or clean?

   d. **Write a short essay or discuss** to agree or disagree:

       i. Wearing shoes in the house is bad for your health.

**Daily
Life** · *Toilet Trouble*

The Situation:

You're at a party at a small but cool club. You're having a great time enjoying some music and drinks. Suddenly, you need to use the toilet but unfortunately for you the restroom of your gender is closed.

The Dilemma:

COULD YOU EVER BE DESPERATE ENOUGH TO GO INTO AN OPPOSITE-GENDER RESTROOM?

1. What Would You Do? (Explain your reasoning)

    a. Use the opposite-gender restroom?

    b. Go outside on the street?

    c. Leave to go to a different club or bathroom?

    d. _____ ?

2. Variables: How would it change the situation if...

    a. you were very young or very old?

    b. the club is very busy or nearly empty?

    c. you are waiting with a friend?

    d. you have to pee or poop?

    e. _____

3. Expansion Activities for Discussion and Writing:

    a. Have you ever been in this situation before? If so, what did you do?

    b. How do you feel about young boys going into public bathrooms with their mothers or young girls going into public bathrooms with their fathers? At what ages is this appropriate or inappropriate?

    c. What do you think about bathroom attendants? Is this job important?

    d. **Write about or discuss** your answers to any of the following issues:

       i. Having more female than male bathrooms available in busy public spaces?

       ii. Universal single bathrooms for all genders?

Daily Life   · *Wild Child*

The Situation:

You're trying to enjoy a meal at a casual restaurant. At the next table, a young child of around six is behaving very badly. They are making lots of noise, banging things on the table, yelling, singing, and getting up and running around. It is definitely disrupting your meal. Their parents seem too busy on their phones and the staff hasn't said anything.

The Dilemma:

WHAT DO YOU DO ABOUT THE CHILD'S ANNOYING BEHAVIOR?

1. What Would You Do? (Explain your reasoning)

   a. Tell the child to behave correctly?

   b. Talk to his parents?

   c. Talk to the staff?

   d. Do nothing and just be patient?

   e. _____?

2. Variables: How would it change the situation if…

   a. the child is younger or older (under 4 or over 10?)

   b. the child is a boy or a girl?

   c. the restaurant is very fancy? Or very cheap?

   d. the child has a physical or mental disability?

   e. _____

3. Expansion Activities for Discussion and Writing

   a. Has this ever happened to you before? If so, what happened? Did you or anyone else say something?

   b. Do you think restaurants or shops should be able to make noisy families leave? Why or why not?

   c. Were your parents strict or lenient? Did you behave well at public places?

   d. How about as a parent? If you had children (or if you have them now), how would you react if your children weren't behaving well at a public place?

   e. What manners are most important to teach children? Why?

   f. **Write about or discuss** the meaning and your reaction to one of the following statements:

      i. Good manners maketh man.

      ii. Young children should be allowed to play free.

Technology & Future · *Clones!*

The Situation:

Good news! You've been chosen to test exciting new technology...making clones! A research group is prepared to make up to five perfect clones of you! They will all have the same memories and look exactly the same except for a small tattoo with their number. You can also give this opportunity to someone else you know instead!

The Dilemma:

DO YOU WANT TO HAVE CLONES OF YOURSELF? IF SO, HOW MANY?

1. What Would You Do? (Explain your reasoning)

a. Go for the maximum: five clones of yourself?

b. Choose fewer than five clones?

c. Give the opportunity to someone else you know?

d. Reject the opportunity entirely?

e. _____

2. Variables: How would it change the situation if…

a. you have to pay $50,000 for each clone?

b. the clones won't have your memories?

c. your friend/family/partner wants you to clone them instead?

d. you can clone anyone you want and make them believe anything?

e. _____

3. Expansion Activities for Discussion and Writing

a. Do you think human cloning will be possible in the future? What are the benefits? What are the drawbacks?

b. Would you ever be willing to clone a favorite pet? Why or why not?

c. Which celebrity would you choose if you could make a clone of anyone to be your:

   i.   partner

   ii.   best friend

   iii.   business partner

d. Read the following quote and Write or Discuss: Which of the two types of cloning do you agree or disagree with? Why?

"There are two kinds of cloning right now. One is therapeutic cloning which is for coming up with cures for life threatening, really, really awful diseases. Then there is reproductive cloning, which is to make a human being out of your DNA and a donor egg"

— Mary Tyler Moore, actress (in an interview with Larry King)

Technology & Future

Explicit

Robot Companion

The Situation:

You are living alone and feeling a bit lonely after a bad breakup. Your parents decide to surprise you with an unusual and very new type of birthday present—a robot partner! This robot is programmed to be the perfect friend, partner, or even boyfriend or girlfriend! It can change both its behavior and appearance to match what's most appealing to you. Your parents think this robot partner can really help you feel less lonely for a short time, or even on a long-term basis, so you give it a try! The robot looks almost human and can do pretty much anything you can imagine. You never have any conflicts! It seems like the perfect partner.

Then one day you meet a very nice person that you really like at a nearby café. You decide it may be time to date a human again. You go out a few times and really enjoy being with this person, though unlike your robot you sometimes disagree and don't get along.

Over all, everything is going well until you bring them home and they meet the robot. They demand you get rid of it immediately or they will break up with you!

The Dilemma:

CAN A ROBOT BE A ROMANTIC PARTNER FOR A HUMAN?

1. What Would You Do? (Explain your reasoning)

a. Get rid of the robot so you can continue dating your new human partner?

b. Refuse to get rid of the robot but try to convince your human partner to accept it?

c. Refuse to get rid of the robot and break up with your human partner?

d. Give up both and go back to being alone?

e. _____

2. Variables: How would it change the situation if...

a. you are truly in love with your human partner

    i.   and they treat you very well?

    ii.   but your friends and family say they don't treat you well?

b. no one else you know has a robot partner?

c. your friends or family also have robot partners?

d. your robot partner can produce children?

e. _____ ?

3. Expansion Activities for Discussion and Writing:

a. Do you think this situation could ever be possible? Why or why not?

b. What are the advantages or disadvantages of having a romantic robot partner?

c. What would an ideal robot partner be able to do? Describe a robot partner that you think people would be willing to buy.

d. Do you think a robot could be an effective parent? Why or why not?

e. **Write a short essay or discuss** whether you agree or disagree with the following statements:

    i.   A robot can never truly love.

    ii.   Humans are too selfish to live together.

    iii.   Humans and robots being together is against nature.

    iv.   Humans and robots being together could be the next step in our evolution.

Technology & Future ·

Spotless Mind Erasing

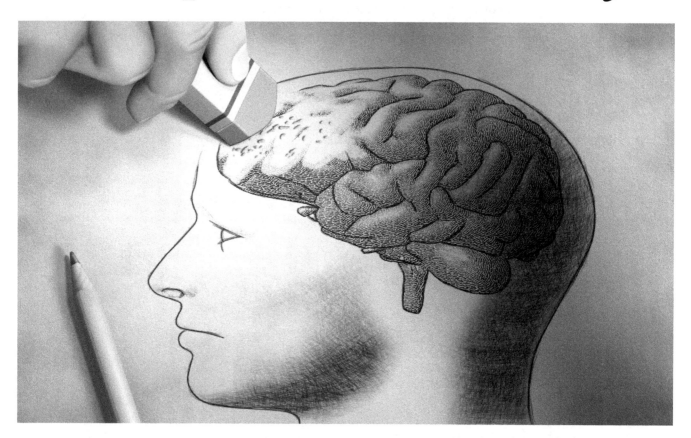

The Situation:

A new company has just opened that has the ability to erase any bad or painful memories. You've just had a very painful breakup with your partner and you are having a hard time getting over it. Your friends all thought it was a bad relationship with very rocky and difficult times, so they are happy for it to be over. Now your parents want to pay for you to have these bad memories erased.

The Dilemma:

ARE WE BETTER OFF WITHOUT OUR PAINFUL MEMORIES?

1. What Would You Do? (Explain your reasoning)

a. Have the painful memories of your breakup erased?

b. Keep your painful memories and refuse to have them erased?

c. _____

2. Variables: How would it change the situation if...

a. you really loved your ex-partner but they cheated on you?

b. you were the one that cheated on your partner?

c. the relationship was really happy but now you're too depressed that it's over?

d. your ex-partner has already had the memory of your relationship erased?

e. instead of a bad relationship, you'd like to erase...

    i.   a terrible accident?

    ii.   an embarrassing moment?

    iii.   a really boring class or job?

    iv.   _____

f. instead of erasing a memory, you can add a false memory, one that will feel real! What kind of false memory would you add?

    i.   a different end to the relationship?

    ii.   an amazing holiday or trip?

    iii.   _____

g. _____

3. Expansion Activities for Discussion and Writing

a. Do you think erasing or changing memories will ever be possible? Why or why not?

b. Have you seen memory erasing in any movies or TV shows?

c. If you could have any memory erased, what would it be?

d. If you could have any type of memory added or changed, what would it be?

e. **Write about or discuss** your answer to one of the following:

    i.   We need some painful memories to teach us to be better people.

    ii.   Painful memories can make us too afraid to take risks.

**Technology &
Future** ·

Teleportation

The Situation:

An amazing thing has just been developed
— a teleportation machine. This allows
the ability to travel anywhere instantly!
Unfortunately, travel is very expensive, more
than you could usually afford! But were
lucky enough to win a special one-hour
round-trip ticket! The problem is you can't
decide where to go! You are currently living
abroad, studying in another country on your
own. Should you visit your family, friends, a
romantic partner, or do something else?

The Dilemma:

**WHERE WOULD YOU GO IF YOU
COULD VISIT ANY PLACE OR
PERSON RIGHT NOW?**

1. What Would You Do?

a. Visit your parents back in your hometown?

b. Visit your friends at an amazing beach party?

c. Meet your girlfriend/boyfriend for a romantic dinner?

d. Visit a famous landmark or museum?

e. _____

2. Variables: How would it change the situation if…

a. your parents/friends/girlfriend/boyfriend don't know you are coming?

b. you just broke up with your girlfriend/boyfriend?

c. today is the last game of an important sports game (such as the World Cup, the Olympics, or the finals)?

d. a friend or family member needs your help?

e. _____

3. Expansion Activities for Discussion and Writing

a. Do you think teleportation will ever be possible? Why or why not?

b. Have you seen teleportation used in any movies or TV shows? If so, how did the people use it? Where did they go?

c. What are the benefits of teleportation? What are the drawbacks?

d. If you could teleport anywhere right this second, where would you go? Why?

e. Plan the perfect day! Create a travel plan!

    i. Imagine you can visit three different places anywhere in the world in 24 hours!

f. **Write about or discuss** one of the following topics:

    i. Teleportation would have more benefits than drawbacks.

    ii. Teleportation will destroy our ability to control our borders.

**Fantasy &
Magic** ·

Gender Switch

The Situation:

There is a new invention: a machine that allows a person to change their gender instantly and painlessly! It's a very popular but expensive process. But you have won a ticket for a free gender change in a random lottery! Once you change, you will be able to change back, but you will have to wait at least one year. If you want to stay as the other gender, you can stay forever! If you are not interested, there are lots of other people who would kill for the chance!

The Dilemma:

WOULD YOU CHANGE YOUR GENDER, EVEN TEMPORARILY?

1. What Would You Do? (Explain your reasoning)

a. Use the machine and change your gender for one year?

b. Use the machine and change your gender forever?

c. Sell your ticket to someone else?

d. Give your ticket to someone you know?

e. Throw the ticket away?

f. _____

2. Variables: How would it change the situation if...

a. you could only change your gender for one day?

b. you could sell the ticket for one million dollars?

c. you and your romantic partner could do the change together?

d. you won't be able to change back?

e. your best friend/family member is begging you for the ticket but doesn't have any money to pay you?

f. instead of gender, you could change your *age*?

g. _____

3. Expansion Activities for Discussion and Writing:

a. Do you think this situation will ever be possible? Why or why not?

b. What are the unique pressures and or/challenges of being...

    i. a man?

    ii. a woman?

    iii. gay?

    iv. transgender?

c. Are men and women's bodies different? Does that affect their personality? In what ways?

d. Are men and women's minds different? Does that affect their personality? In what ways?

e. **Write about or discuss** one of the following:

    i. Men and women are equal in every way.

    ii. Women are weaker than men and require more protection.

    iii. Women should serve in the military equally with men.

    iv. Men are not as mature and socially skilled as women.

    v. Women are kinder and less violent than men.

Fantasy & Magic · *Live Forever*

The Situation:

You have discovered something amazing: the real fountain of youth!

By drinking the water from this magical well, you can make yourself younger, or even live forever! Every sip will add ten years to your life and you will stay healthy at your current age. If you drink a full gallon (four liters), you will live forever!

Unfortunately, once you drink the water the effects cannot be reversed. Also, the fountain will disappear and you will not be able to use it again.

The Dilemma:

HOW LONG WILL YOU CHOOSE TO LIVE?

1. What Would You Do? (Explain your reasoning)

   a. Drink the full gallon (four liters) and live forever?

   b. Drink the well, but less than the full amount?

   c. Not drink from the well?

   d. Let a family or friend use the well instead?

   e. _____

2. Variables: How would it change the situation if...

   a. you are 80 years old?

   b. you are 10 years old?

   c. each sip of the fountain can make you 1 year younger?

   d. your family or friend is dying!

   e. _____

3. Expansion Activities for Discussion and Writing:

   a. Do you think we will be able to make people younger in the future? Why or why not?

   b. If you could live forever, what age would you like to be? Why?

   c. **Write a short essay or discuss** your answer if you agree or disagree:

   i.   According to a study carried out by the London School of Economics and Political Science, happiness peaks at two ages: 23 and 69[1]

---

1 Siofra Brennan, "Revealed: The two surprising ages when we're at our HAPPIEST (and why it's bad news if you're in your middle years)." *Daily Mail,* 15 April 2017 https://www.dailymail.co.uk/femail/article-4405834/The-two-ages-happiness-peaks-adult-life.html.

**Fantasy &
Magic** · *Read My Mind*

The Situation:

One day after bumping your head, you discover something amazing — you can read anyone's mind! Sadly, this ability will only last one day, but maybe that's more than enough! What are your parents, friends, even strangers thinking? Now you can know everything but maybe too much?

The Dilemma:

HOW DO YOU USE YOUR NEW POWERS OF TELEPATHY? WHAT'S THE MOST IMPORTANT THING YOU WOULD DO?

1. What Would You Do? (Explain your reasoning)

a. Read the mind of a girl or boy you like to get them to like you?

b. Use your power to win at gambling?

c. Win any argument with your parents?

d. Become a perfect student?

e. Try to block your power out of fear?

f. _____

2. Variables: How would it change the situation if…

a. you can only read only one person's mind? Who would you choose?

b. you can teach others how to get this mind-reading power for one day? Who would you teach how to use this power to?

c. you have the power forever? What kind of job would you get?

d. every time you read someone's mind, they can read yours too?

e. _____

3. Expansion Activities for Discussion and Writing:

a. Do you think this situation could ever be possible? Why or why not?

b. Have you seen or heard of any real people that can read minds? Do you think this is possible or is it a trick?

c. Do you think it is *ethical* to read someone's mind?

   i.   Why or why not?

d. **Write a short essay or discuss** if you agree or disagree with the following expression:

   i.   People are islands: even the closest family or friends never truly know what another is thinking.

Politics · *If I Were President*

The Situation:

The United States holds a special new election for president. They decide to choose the winner at random. And guess what? The winner is you! The big question is, what do you want to do first?

The Dilemma:

WHAT WOULD YOU DO AS LEADER OF A COUNTRY?

1. What Would You Do? (Explain your reasoning)

a. Lower taxes for everyone?

b. Give free healthcare to everyone?

c. Focus on finding jobs for everyone?

d. Protect the environment?

e. Take military action against a dangerous country?

f. _____

2. Variables: How would it change the situation if...

a. more than 50% of the public support you and are happy to have you in office?

b. less than 50% of the public support you and are happy to have you in office?

c. America is currently at war?

d. the economy is doing very well?

e. the economy is doing very poorly?

f. you became the leader of your country?

g. _____

3. Expansion Activities for Discussion and Writing:

a. Do you think you could ever be a political leader? Why or why not?

b. Think of presidents or leaders in real life. What issues do they focus on? Do you agree with their actions?

c. Can you think of any presidents or leaders from TV shows or movies? What did they focus on? Do you agree with their actions or not?

d. **Write a short essay or discuss** the following:

   i. What should be a leader's main responsibilities?

   ii. What's the difference between a good and bad leader?

   iii. Who is one of the greatest or worst leaders in history?

Money & Possessions · *Lucky Lotto*

The Situation:

You did it! You've won the National Lottery playing your own special numbers! Now you will receive $200 million dollars!

It sounds like great news, but with the money come lots of new challenges as well! Your parents could use help paying for their house. Your brother wants to attend an expensive college. Your best friend's car just broke down. Also, you also have lots of other family members that are very poor.

The Dilemma:

HOW WILL YOU CHOOSE TO SPEND YOUR NEW FORTUNE?

1. What Would You Do? (Explain your reasoning)

a. spend all of the money on yourself?

b. share the money with all of your family and friends?

c. only share money with friends and family who really need it?

d. save all of the money for the future?

e. give the winning ticket to someone else?

f. _____

2. Variables: How would it change the situation if...

a. you are...

    i. rich? (You make more than 1 million a year?)

    ii. VERY rich (you make more than 20 million a year?)

    iii. very poor (you have no job!)

b. you have to choose how to receive the money, either:

    i. take all the money now (but pay a 50% tax!)

    ii. get paid $20 million once a year, minus a 20% tax for 10 years.

c. your romantic partner wants you to split it with them or they will break up with you?

d. a criminal group such as the Mafia says you must give them half of the money or they will kill you?

e. The money is cursed, and if you take it you will die in exactly 20 years?

f. _____ ?

3. Expansion Activities for Discussion and Writing:

    a. Have you, or anyone you know, ever won a lottery before?

        i. If so, how much did you win? What did you spend it on?

    b. If you won a lot of money…

        i. What would be the first thing you would spend it on?

        ii. What is something you definitely wouldn't spend it on?

    c. According to an article in *Time Magazine*, nearly 70% of lottery winners lose ALL of their winnings in just a few years[2].

        i. Why do you think this is?

        ii. What are the biggest challenges of keeping your lottery winnings?

    d. Write a short essay or discuss your answer to one of the following:

        i. Money can solve all of your problems.

        ii. Money: Easy come, easy go.

---

2 Melissa Chan. "Here's How Winning the Lottery Makes You Miserable." *Time*. January 12, 2016. Accessed October 11, 2018. http://time.com/4176128/powerball-jackpot-lottery-winners/.

Ethics · *Meet Your Hero*

The Situation:

You are having a quiet dinner with a friend at a nice, small restaurant. Suddenly, you notice that eating alone is a very famous person. Not only is this person famous, but they are also your hero. You've always wanted to meet them. You want to run over and talk to them immediately, but your friend tells you they might be alone for a reason. Maybe because you like them you shouldn't bother them.

The Dilemma:

DO CELEBRITIES DESERVE PRIVACY?

1. What Would You Do? (Explain your reasoning)

a. Go to the celebrity's table and talk to them?

b. Wait until the celebrity is leaving and talk to them then?

c. Respect the celebrity's privacy?

d. _____

2. Variables: How would it change the situation if...

a. the celebrity is with a big group?

b. the celebrity is having a romantic dinner with one other person?

c. lots of other people are bothering the celebrity?

d. the celebrity is your friend's hero?

e. the celebrity has a reputation for being...

    i. very nice to fans?

    ii. very mean to fans?

f. _____

3. Expansion Activities for Discussion and Writing:

a. Have you or anyone you know met someone famous before? Who was it? What was their reaction?

b. Do you think it's ok to bother celebrities in public? Why or why not?

c. If you were famous, how would you feel about people bothering you in public?

d. What is an example of a famous celebrity with a good reputation with fans?

e. What is an example of a celebrity with a bad reputation with fans?

f. **Write a short essay or discuss** your answer to one of the following statements:

    i. Celebrities have a responsibility to their fans.

    ii. Fans are often disrespectful to celebrities.

Ethics · # Wild Game Safari Hunting

The Situation:

You're in Africa on an exciting sightseeing safari holiday with your friends. You are enjoying seeing so many amazing animals in nature — lions, tigers, elephants, giraffes, and many more interesting types of wildlife!

One day you head out with your friends and the guide has a shocking surprise — a large number of guns in your safari car! The guide says, "Today, you get to go hunting for the wild animal of your choice!"

You are told the guide will help you shoot and kill any animal of your choice, and you will be able to take a picture of your conquest. The guide insists this is a tradition, and you shouldn't be worried because so many animals are hunted or killed by others in the jungle every day. Your friends are all excited and ready to hunt a safari animal… but how about you?

The Dilemma:

CAN YOU HUNT A BEAUTIFUL OR SPECIAL ANIMAL?

1. What Would You Do? (Explain your reasoning)

a. Refuse to join the hunting safari?

b. Refuse and also try to convince your friends not to hunt also?

c. Hunt a...

    i.   tiger or lion?

    ii.   elephant?

    iii. giraffe?

    iv. gorilla

    v.   other _____

d. _____

2. Variables: How would it change the situation if...

a. The animals you are planning to hunt are endangered?

b. The animals you are planning to hunt need to be killed because of overpopulation?

c. The animals you are planning to hunt need to be killed because they are predators that are eating too many other animals (for example, a few tigers are killing all the giraffes?)

d. Instead of friends, your family are with you and they all want to hunt?

e. _____?

3. Expansion Activities for Discussion and Writing

a. Do you think this situation ever happens? Why or why not?

b. Have you ever gone hunting?

    i.   What are some reasons for hunting wild animals?

    ii.   What are some reasons for not hunting wild animals?

c. If you had to go hunting...

    i.   Which animal would you be most willing to hunt?

    ii.   Which animal would you be least willing to hunt?

d. Write a short essay or discuss your answer to agree or disagree with the following statements:

    i.   People who illegally hunt endangered animals should be put in jail.

    ii.   Hunting should be legal as long as you're planning to eat what you hunt.

Ethics · *Foreigner Discrimination*

The Situation:

You are one of the managers at a restaurant looking to hire new staff. You and one other manager are in charge of hiring a new dishwasher and cleaner. Two applicants are interested in the job. One is a young, lazy-looking white teenager looking for a summer job. The other is a dark-skinned man with an accent, who says he needs the job to feed his family, and who's willing to work all hours and days needed. The dark-skinned man is clearly a foreigner, as he doesn't have any of the necessary papers or visas to be hired (This is also called an 'undocumented worker').

One of the managers wants to hire the white teenager, because he's a 'a real American' and because 'illegal aliens shouldn't be in this country!'

The other manager wants to hire the foreigner because he believes he will work much harder, and has to feed his family (and also will be paid under-the-table which will help to avoid taxes!)

They are both looking at you to be the tie-breaker…

The Dilemma:

WHO WOULD YOU CHOOSE FOR THE JOB: THE LAZY TEENAGER OR THE UNDOCUMENTED FOREIGNER?

1. What Would You Do? (Explain your reasoning)

a. Give the job to the teenager?

b. Give the job to the foreigner?

c. _____

2. Variables: How would it change the situation if…

a. you are also from the same country as the foreigner?

b. the foreigner has a visa, but both of the other managers don't want to hire him because they're racist?

c. the American teenager has a criminal record?

d. the American is an adult and has a family also?

e. _____

3. Expansion Activities for Discussion and Writing:

a. Have you ever met someone who was staying in your country illegally? Were they working?

b. Have you ever witnessed discrimination against foreigners…

    i. in your country?

    ii. in another country or city?

c. The following quote is from the poem "The New Colossus" by Emma Lazarus, written on the base of the Statue of Liberty (shown in the picture above): _"Give me your tired, your poor,/ Your huddled masses yearning to breathe free,/ The wretched refuse of your teeming shore."_

    i. What do you think this quote means?

    ii. How does this saying relate to American culture?

    iii. Do you agree or disagree with this saying?

d. **Write about or discuss** the following topic(s):

    i. Businesses shouldn't hire foreign workers who are in the country illegally.

    ii. Foreign workers are vital to make a country stronger.

PART III

SITUATIONS FOR ADULTS

The following situations are designed for adults. Some of the topics are more mature in content and thus more suitable for older learners. There are also more complicated and intricate situations that may require prior knowledge and involve intense ethical dilemmas. Many of these are subjects suitable for additional expansion in writing or even research!

**Friends &
Family** · *Bad Music*

The Situation:

Your 12-year-old child is always listening to loud and aggressive music. They are listening to music in their rooms, walking around with their headphones, in the car, everywhere! The music they listen to often has shocking lyrics that glorify violence and say bad things about women. You hate to hear them play this music from their room, and are worried it might affect their behavior. You want to stop them listening to it somehow, but you don't want to control them.

The Dilemma:

SHOULD YOU, AND HOW CAN YOU, CONTROL YOUR CHILD'S MUSIC HABITS?

1. What Would You Do? (Explain your reasoning)

a. Stop your child from listening to this bad music?

b. Review all the music your child wants to listen to?

c. Set a limit for how much your child can listen to this bad music?

d. Let them enjoy their music freely.

e. _____

2. Variables: How would it change the situation if...

a. your child is...

    i. a boy or girl?

    ii. under 10? over 16?

b. the bad music is...

    i. hip-hop or rap?

    ii. heavy metal?

c. the bad lyrics your child listening to are mostly...

    i. swear words?

    ii. racist?

    iii. sexist?

    iv. misogynist? (bad words about women)

    v. misandrist? (bad words about men)

d. instead of your child, the person who listens to the bad music is...

    i. your best friend?

    ii. your brother or sister?

    iii. your boyfriend or girlfriend?

e. _____

3. Expansion Activities for Discussion and Writing:

a. Did your parents ever try and stop or control your music listening? If so, what did you do?

b. Do you think you might have this conflict with your children someday?

c. What genres of music do you like the most? Which genres do you like the least?

d. **Research and Write**: Answer the following questions:

    i. Listen to a popular song in a genre of music you don't like. Do you dislike the song? Why? Is there anything you like about it?

e. **Discuss or write a short response** to the following music-related statements:

    i. The newest music is never understood by the older generation.

    ii. It's important to let people listen to music that inspires them.

    iii. Music with bad words can damage young people's minds.

Friends & Family · *Child Discipline*

The Situation:

You have two young children, aged four and one. Your four-year-old keeps hitting the one-year-old on the head and you want them to stop their misbehavior. You have warned them several times but they won't listen to you.

The Dilemma:

HOW DO YOU STOP YOUR YOUNG CHILD'S BAD BEHAVIOR?

1. What Would You Do? (Explain your reasoning)

a. Keep telling your child firmly?

b. Put the child in a time-out?

c. Spank the child?

d. Do nothing and just be patient?

e. _____?

2. Variables: How would it change the situation if...

a. the child is under 4? Over 10?

b. the child is a boy? A girl?

c. you are at home? In the car? At a public place?

d. the child has a physical or mental disability?

e. _____

3. Expansion Activities for Discussion and Writing

a. Has this ever happened to before? If so, what happened? Did you or anyone else say something?

b. What did your parents do when you misbehaved? Spankings? Time-outs? Other methods?

c. If you had children, or if you have them now), how would you discipline them?

d. What manners are most important to teach children? Why?

e. **For writing or discussion**: Is corporal punishment, such as spanking or hitting, necessary? Why or why not?

    i.   In school?

    ii.   At home?

    iii.   In the military?

Friends & Family · *Get Off the Phone!*

The Situation:

You gave your 10-year-old a phone so you could contact him at school or for emergencies, and so he could fit in with his friends. But now he's on it on the time! He's even on his phone at the dinner table and in his room late at night . . . And your child is often upset about something a friend said online. You think your child is using his phone way too much but you're not sure what to do?

The Dilemma:

SHOULD YOU LIMIT OR STOP CHILDREN'S PHONE USE?

1. What Would You Do? (Explain your reasoning)

a. Set a daily limit for phone use?

b. Not allow the phone in certain places, such as the bedroom?

c. Not allow the phone to be used in the house?

d. Take the phone away…

   i.   temporarily?

   ii.   permanently?

e. Just ignore the situation, as its normal with kids these days?

f. _____ ?

2. Variables: How would it change the situation if…

a. your child is…

   i.   younger (3-6 years old)

   ii.   a teenager (13-18 years old)

   iii. a boy? A girl?

   iv.   has mental or physical disabilities?

b. it's your younger brother or sister instead?

c. it's your best friend who is using their phone too much?

d. _____

3. Expansion Activities for Discussion and Writing:

a. Have your parents ever tried to limit your phone use? If so, what was your reaction?

b. At what age should a child have a smartphone?

c. At what age are they ready for Social Media?

d. If you were a parent, what apps or programs would you try to limit on your child's phone?

e. **For writing or discussion:** Do you agree or disagree with the following statements?

   i.   Having smartphones is a big advantage for children these days.

   ii.   Smartphones are damaging the younger generations.

Friends & Family · *Sleeping with Baby*

The Situation:

Congratulations! You and your partner
have had your first baby! But now an issue
has come up that you haven't decided yet:
Where will the baby sleep, and for how
long? You have purchased a crib, and put it
in a separate room for the baby. However,
you and your partner have also talked about
some other options. You could put the crib
in your bedroom so the baby is closer and
easier to change or to help in the night.

Or you could go even further with *co-sleeping*,
when the whole family sleeps together with
the baby in your bed. The big question is
what to do and for how long. Is sleeping close
to your baby important? What about the
relationship with you and your partner?

The Dilemma:

**WHERE SHOULD YOUR
BABY SLEEP?**

1. What Would You Do? (Explain your reasoning)

a. Have your baby sleep in their crib in another room?

b. Have your baby sleep in their crib in the same room?

c. Co-sleep with your baby for a short time, 6 months or less, and then move them in to their own room?

d. Co-sleep with your baby until they start elementary school (~6 years old)

e. _____

2. Variables: How would it change the situation if...

a. Your partner really wants to put the baby in another room because they don't want to lose private time with you?

b. Your partner wants to co-sleep with the baby and no longer seems romantically interested in you?

c. Your baby was *premature* (born early) and needs extra care for at least a few months?

d. Your mother (or your partner's mother) wants to stay at your house and help with the baby for a while?

e. You or your partner has a very busy job with long hours?

f. _____

3. Expansion Activities for Discussion and Writing:

a. Do you know where you slept when you were a baby?

    i.   If you co-slept, do you think it was a good idea?

b. Has someone you know been in this situation before?

c. Which of the following do you think you'd do in the future if you have a baby?

    i.   co-sleeping?

    ii.   crib in another room?

    iii.   crib in the same room?

d. **Write or Discuss a short response to these statements:** In many parts of the world, co-sleeping is very common, though it is much rarer in the US and some Western Countries.

    i.   Is co-sleeping a good idea? Why or why not?

    ii.   In some countries, co-sleeping until the child starts elementary school (~6 years old) is also common. Do you think this is a good idea? Why or why not?

**Love &
Relationships**

Explicit

Cheating Partner

The Situation:

Your longtime partner has been on a trip and you haven't seen them for weeks. You've missed them terribly! When you pick them up, they seem strangely distant. After you've gone home and talked a bit, they reveal that they cheated on you with someone else on their trip. It was an affair that lasted a couple weeks, but now they're finished and they want to be with only you…

The Dilemma:

CAN YOU FORGIVE A CHEATING PARTNER THAT YOU LOVE?

1. What Would You Do? (Explain your reasoning)

a. Forgive your partner and trust that it won't have them again?

b. Forgive them but distrust them and watch them carefully?

c. Stay with your partner, but have your own affair?

    i.   In secret?

    ii.   Tell your partner for revenge?

d. Break up with your partner?

e. _____ ?

2. Variables: How would it change the situation if...

a. you are married?

    i.   with children?

    ii.   without children?

b. you tell your best friend(s) who says you should

    i.   break up

    ii.   stay together

c. your partner says this situation made them realize how much they love you, and they ask to marry you?

d. Your partner won't stop the affair and wants to have an open relationship?

e. _____

3. Expansion Activities for Discussion and Writing:

a. Have you ever been in a situation like this before? If so, what did you do?

b. Has anyone else you know been in this situation?

c. Have you seen a movie or TV show or read a book about an affair? What happened?

d. **Write a short essay or discuss whether you agree or disagree** with the following statements:

    i.   Once a cheater, always a cheater.

    ii.   If you love someone, let them go free. If they come back to you, it's true love.

Love & Relationships · *Friends Fighting*

The Situation:

Two of your best friends have been in a relationship together for years. They are both great friends of yours, but they always seem to be fighting when together. They argue and fight so much that you and others are starting to avoid meeting them. Everyone, including their own parents, thinks they should break up!

The Dilemma:

SHOULD YOU CONVINCE YOUR FRIENDS TO BREAK UP?

1. What Would You Do? (Explain your reasoning)

    a. Talk to both of them together about breaking up?

    b. Talk to one or both of your friends separately about breaking up?

    c. Try to work with one or both of them at getting along better.

    d. Ignore the situation and hope they break up on their own!

    e. _____?

2. Variables: How would it change the situation if...

    a. you know one (or both) is hitting the other?

    b. you know one (or both) is cheating on their partner?

    c. you are only friends with one of them?

    d. you are the one in the difficult relationship and your friends tell YOU to break up?

    e. _____

3. Expansion Activities for Discussion and Writing:

    a. Have you ever been in a situation like this before? If so, what did you do?

    b. Has anyone else you know been in this situation?

    c. Have you seen this type of situation in a movie or TV show or read about one in a book?

    d. How can tell if your friends/family are in a bad romantic relationship?

    e. How can tell if your friends/family are in a good romantic relationship?

    f. **Write a short essay or discuss** the following question:

        i. Which is more important, a good friend or a romantic partner?

Love & Relationships · *Love Inequality*

The Situation:

You have been with your partner for a few years now. You love them very much and often tell them how much you care, buy them presents, and do everything you can to make them happy. But they've always been a bit cold with you. They will only say "I love you" if you say it first, and they always seem hesitant when they do. Your friends think you love your partner much more than they love you. When you try to talk about it, they change the subject. It's really starting to bother you…

The Dilemma:

DOES LOVE ALWAYS HAVE TO BE EQUAL?

1. What Would You Do? (Explain your reasoning)

a. Break up with your partner?

b. Act colder with your partner and hope they start to appreciate you more?

c. Make a list of things you would like your partner to do to show their love?

d. Stay with your partner, but have an affair?

    i.   In secret?

    ii.   Tell your partner for revenge?

e. Break up with your partner?

f. _____?

2. Variables: How would it change the situation if...

a. your partner is...

    i.   10 or more years older?

    ii.   10 or more years younger?

b. your best friend says you should...

    i.   break up?

    ii.   stay together?

c. you are married?

    i.   with children?

    ii.   without children?

d. _____

3. Expansion Activities for Discussion and Writing:

a. Have you ever been in a situation like this before?

    i.   If so, what did you do?

    ii.   Has anyone else you known been in this situation?

    iii.   Have you seen this type of situation in a movie/book/TV show? How was the situation similar or different to real life?

b. Is it possible for a couple to love each other equally? Why or why not?

c. Would you rather be in a relationship where…

    i.   you love the other person more?

    ii.   the other person loves you more?

d. **Write a short essay or discuss whether you agree or disagree** with this statement:

    i.   It is better to love than to be loved.

**Love &
Relationships**
Explicit

Mile High Club

The Situation:

You're on a long airplane ride with your partner. They suddenly suggest something very crazy but exciting — to join the Mile High Club! They want to go to the restroom together and have a bit of romantic time! You are nervous about this, but you partner says "YOLO! You only live once".

The Dilemma:

HOW DO YOU FEEL ABOUT ROMANTIC BEHAVIOR IN INAPPROPRIATE PLACES?

1. What Would You Do? (Explain your reasoning)

a. Agree with your partner and go to the airplane restroom together?

b. Try to talk your partner out of it?

c. Outright refuse to go?

d. _____ ?

2. Variables: How would it change the situation if...

a. you are in a different location?

    i.   on a bus or train?

    ii.   at a fancy restaurant?

    iii.   at your friends or your partner's parents' house?

    iv.   _____

b. your partner did this before with their ex?

    i.   the plane is...

    ii.   full?

    iii.   almost empty?

c. _____

3. Expansion Activities for Discussion and Writing:

a. Have you ever been in a situation like this before?

    i.   If so, what did you do?

    ii.   Do you know anyone who has been in this situation?

    iii.   Have you seen this situation in a TV show or movie?

b. Are you usually open to taking risks?

    i.   In the past, were you or your _____ more likely to be the risk-taker?
- Partners.
- Siblings.
- Friends.

c. What are your biggest turn-ons in dating?

    i.   Looks (size, facial features, muscle, etc.)

    ii.   Personality (kind, funny, decisive, etc.)

    iii.   Something else _____

d. **Write a short essay** to define this statement and whether you agree or disagree:
YOLO - You Only Live Once

Love & Relationships
Explicit

Post-Marital Intimacy

The Situation:

You are your partner have had a wonderful romance! After spending several years together, you got married. After that your intimacy started to decline. And then you had children which made it even harder to be intimate. Once you had an intense romantic life, traveling and going out together, and having lots of intimate time. Now your partner says things have changed. "We are parents now, not lovers." They want to focus on the kids, and don't believe spending time or intimacy is important. They tell you that after the kids are older, things may change. This is difficult for you, because you're not sure if this is something you can accept!

The Dilemma:

HOW MUCH INTIMACY IS NECESSARY IN MARRIAGE?

1. What Would You Do? (Explain your reasoning)

a. Agree with your partner and focus on your family life and forget about intimacy or romance?

b. Try and negotiate with your partner to arrange some private time or intimacy?

c. Threaten to leave your partner if they no longer want to be intimate?

d. Ask your friends or family for advice and follow what they say?

e. _____ ?

2. Variables: How would it change the situation if your partner...

a. refuses to spend ANY private time with you?

b. refuses to be intimate with you?

c. says they no longer love you?

d. tells you that you are allowed to have an affair?

e. is the one pressuring you to spend more private or intimate time and is ignoring the children too much?

f. _____

3. Expansion Activities for Discussion and Writing:

a. Have you or someone you know been in a situation like this before?

  i. If so, what did you do?

  ii. Have you seen this situation on a TV show or movie?

b. How do you think a couple's relationship changes after marriage? How about after children?

c. In many parts of the world (but rarely in the US) marriage is considered more of a business agreement, and post-marital romance or intimacy is rare or non-existent.

  i. Is this true in your culture?

  ii. Is the Western attitude, which prioritizes romance and companionship, in some ways selfish?

d. **Write a short essay or discuss whether you agree or disagree** with one of the following statements:

  i. Romance in all relationships will decline after marriage and children.

  ii. It is necessary to keep romance alive in all marriages.

Love & Relationships · *Value Differences*

The Situation:

You and your partner are in a wonderful romantic relationship. You get along very well and are deeply in love. You are ready to ask them to marry you, but there is one issue in the way: Your partner is very religious in a very small minor religion. Because of this, your partner has some unusual beliefs and every weekend they go to a strange church. You're also unsure if both of your families will be ok with the differences in your religious values, as many people would think their religion is "strange."

The Dilemma:

CAN YOU MARRY SOMEONE WITH DIFFERENT VALUES SUCH AS BELONGING TO A DIFFERENT RELIGION?

1. What Would You Do? (Explain your reasoning)

    a. Ask your partner to marry and not worry about the religious differences?

    b. Ask your partner to marry, but only if they change their religion?

    c. Break up with your partner if they won't change?

    d. Change to your partner's religion so you can get married more easily?

    e. _____ ?

2. Variables: How would it change the situation if...

    a. your partner's religion is...

        i. Christian?

        ii. Muslim?

        iii. Buddhist?

        iv. Scientologist?

        v. Other _____

    b. you are the one that is more religious and your partner wants to stop you from practicing your beliefs?

    c. your partner is an atheist who doesn't believe in any god?

    d. instead of religious differences, your partner is very...

        i. liberal?

        ii. conservative?

    e. your parents forbid you to marry this person?

    f. _____

3. Expansion Activities for Discussion and Writing:

    a. Have you ever been in a situation like this before?

        i. Have you dated someone from a different religion?

        ii. Have you had a close friend from another religion?

    b. If you truly love someone with another religious belief, could you convert to their religion to marry them? Why or why not?

    c. Besides religion, what other beliefs/differences could be a problem with romantic partners or friends?

    d. **Write a short essay or discuss whether you agree or disagree** with this famous quote:

"Passion is universal humanity. Without it, religion, history, romance and art would be useless." –Honore de Balzac, author

Daily Life · *Bathroom Friendly*

The Situation:

You work at a small but very busy café. One morning before work, your manager announces a very important meeting. It seems there are some issues with the bathrooms getting busy. Currently, there are separate one-person bathrooms for each gender, but many women have complained that at busy times of day, there can be a long line for the women's room and no line at all for the men's room! In addition, some transgender customers have complained that having restricted bathrooms is discrimination. On other hand, some of the men at the café have complained that women take too long in the bathroom and they want to keep their own bathroom.

Your manager has allowed the decision to come down to a vote, (there are four men and four women at the café) and it is tied! All have voted...except for you!

The Dilemma:

HOW DO YOU PROVIDE EQUAL BATHROOM OPPORTUNITIES?

1. What Would You Do? (Explain your reasoning)

a. Vote to make both bathrooms universal?

b. Vote to keep separate men's and women's bathroom?

c. Ask the women and vote with their decision?

d. Ask the men and vote with their decision?

e. _____

2. Variables: How would it change the situation if...

a. the staff at the café were...

    i. all men?

    ii. all women?

b. you took a poll of the customers to decide and the majority chose...

    i. universal bathrooms?

    ii. separate men's and women's bathrooms?

c. the café were...

    i. very fancy and expensive?

    ii. cheap and casual?

d. _____

3. Expansion Activities for Discussion and Writing:

a. Have you (or someone you know) ever been in a situation like this before?

b. Do women use the restroom more than men? If so, why do you think this is?

c. Are the reasons why men and women use the restroom different sometimes?

d. Are men or women more likely to go to the bathroom in groups? Why do you think this is?

e. Do you think businesses should provide bathroom options for individuals who don't identify as a single gender? Why or why not?

f. **Write a short essay or discuss** if you agree or disagree with the following famous sayings:

    i. Restroom opportunities are often unfair for women at public places.

    ii. It discriminates against men to give women equal access to restroom facilities.

Daily Life · # *Workplace Lies*

The Situation:

You're applying for the perfect job. It has good hours, a great salary, and the work fits exactly your interest! You're having a great interview, until they start to ask you some questions about work experience that you don't have. They tell you they will only hire you if you have this experience…

The Dilemma:

WOULD YOU LIE TO GET YOUR DREAM JOB?

1. What Would You Do? (Explain your reasoning)

a. Lie and say you have the experience to get the job?

b. Tell the truth about your experience and lose the job?

c. _____

2. Variables: How would it change the situation if...

a. you have a family and children at home to take care of so you need the job?

b. your partner says they will break up with you if you don't get the job?

c. you will have to move back home with your parents if you don't get the job?

d. you are competing for the job with your...

    i. best friend?

    ii. sibling?

e. _____

3. Expansion Activities for Discussion and Writing:

a. Have you or someone you know ever been in a situation like this before? If so, did you or they get the job?

b. Is it okay to lie about, or not tell, the following at a job interview?

    i. age

    ii. relationship status (single/married/divorced/etc.)

    iii. medical history

    iv. drinking/smoking/drug use?

    v. other _____

c. If you are the manager interviewing someone for a job...

    i. What two questions are most important to ask?

    ii. What two questions would be inappropriate to ask?

d. Write a short essay or discuss if you agree or disagree with the following statements:

    i. It's impossible to truly succeed unless you're willing to lie, cheat, or steal.

    ii. The truth costs nothing, but a lie can cost your everything.

**Technology &
Future/Politics** · *Overpopulation*

The Situation:

It's the future and the planet is extremely
overcrowded. In order to have enough
resources for humans, a controversial new
law has been passed: People can only live
until the age of 40. At 40, all humans are
given two choices: to go to a special *Wellness
Center* where they will have a peaceful death,
or to be relocated. If they choose *relocation,*
they will get on a spaceship and be sent to
live in a dome on the Moon or Mars. So far,
the plan has worked well, with a healthy
young Earth population. But now you are 39
and approaching your 40th birthday…

The Dilemma:

**WILL YOU CHOOSE AN EARLY
DEATH OR AN UNCERTAIN
NEW LIFE?**

1. What Would You Do? (Explain your reasoning)

    a. Take a spaceship and live in a dome on Mars or the Moon?

    b. Choose the "wellness" option and end your life early?

    c. Go talk to your friends or family and follow their advice?

    d. Try to hide and avoid having to make a choice?

    e. Try to talk to the government about changing this plan?

    f. _____

2. Variables: How would it change the situation if...

    a. you have many friends and family on Mars or the Moon?

    b. you don't have any friends or family on Mars or the Moon?

    c. instead of 40 years old, the maximum Earth age is...

        i. younger?

        ii. older?

    d. the only choice once you're 40 is...

        i. death?

        ii. a forcible move to Mars or the Moon?

    e. your friends

        i. think you should accept the proposal?

        ii. think you shouldn't accept the proposal?

    f. instead of age, the reason for deciding who to relocate is...

        i. size — people who are too big

        ii. health —people who have serious illnesses?

        iii. Education—people with the lowest scores on a test?

        iv. personality— people with less empathy?

        v. background—people with criminal backgrounds?

        vi. _____

    g. _____?

3. Expansion Activities for Discussion and Writing:

    a. Do you think a similar situation could ever be possible? Why or why not?

    b. Do you think overpopulation will be a serious issue in the future? Why or why not?

        i. What are the biggest challenges that overpopulation will create?

    c. What other problems do you think humans will face in the next 20 years?

    d. Write a short essay or discuss your answer to the following question:

        i. What are some solutions to overpopulation in the future?

Robot Work Partner

The Situation:

Your job is very busy and you usually rely on your partners, John and Sarah, to help you do your job. You also have a nice, friendly relationship and.enjoy having the occasional lunch with them.

One day you come to work to find a big surprise. Instead of your old partners, you find a robot! "This is the newest robot work model," your boss tells you. "He can do everything John and Sarah did and a lot more!"

You quickly discover that your boss is right. The robot can do any kind of work, even tell jokes and give back rubs. Your work is getting done faster than ever!

After a few weeks, John and Sarah contact you about joining them together at a new company! You miss the human interaction but you're really not sure if you want to go!

The Dilemma:

CAN A ROBOT BE AS GOOD A WORK PARTNER AS A HUMAN?

1. What Would You Do? (Explain your reasoning)

a. Join Sarah and John at the new company?

b. Stay with your job and your new robot partner?

c. Talk to your boss about bringing Sarah and John back to your company?

d. _____

2. Variables: How would it change the situation if...

a. your salary will be higher if you work with the robot partner?

b. you find either John or Sarah very attractive, but they're also terrible at doing their job?

c. your boss is also replaced by a robot?

d. your robot partner watches you and criticizes your performance?

e. your robot partner makes lots of mistakes?

f. _____ ?

3. Expansion Activities for Discussion and Writing:

a. Do you think this situation could ever be possible? Why or why not?

b. What are the advantages and disadvantages of robots doing human jobs?

c. What kinds of job do you think robots can most easily replace humans in?

    i.   now?

    ii.   in the future?

d. Would you be willing to trust a…

    i.   robot salesperson?

    ii.   robot doctor?

    iii.   robot lawyer?

e. **Write a short essay or discuss** your answer to agree or disagree with the following statements:

    i.   Robots being able to do more jobs will make our lives better.

    ii.   Robots taking human jobs will be a huge crisis in the future.

Technology & Future ·

Smart Self-Driving Car

The Situation:

You are a judge deciding a very difficult case. A self-driving car hit and killed a pedestrian who was walking across the street. At the time, the driver was sleeping behind the wheel, so they weren't aware of what the car was doing. Adding to the complications, the car chose to hit the pedestrian because they were crossing the street during a red light. The car's computer calculated there wasn't enough time to hit the brakes, and swerving might have caused a bigger accident with more deaths or injuries.

The Dilemma:

CAN WE TRUST SELF-DRIVING CARS TO MAKE LIFE-AND-DEATH DECISIONS?

1. What Would You Do? (Explain your reasoning)

    a. Rule that the driver must pay the family for the wrongful death.

        i.   Would you send the driver to jail?

    b. Rule that the car company must pay the family for the wrongful death.

        i.   Would you send the designer of the technology to jail?

    c. Rule on the side of the car company and driver?

    d. Rule that self-driving cars should not make these kinds of decisions?

    e. _____

2. Variables: How would it change the situation if...

    a. the pedestrian was...

        i.   a child?

        ii.   an old man or woman?

        iii.   using drugs or alcohol?

    b. the driver was

        i.   a tired family man or woman with a busy schedule?

        ii.   a teenager using drugs or alcohol?

    c. the computer in the car wasn't able to see the pedestrian due to technological failure?

    d. the driver's car was the only self-driving car on the road?

    e. all of the cars on the road were self-driving?

    f. _____ ?

3. Expansion Activities for Discussion and Writing:

    a. Do you think this situation could ever be possible? Why or why not?

    b. How do you feel about self-driving cars? Would you like to use one? Why or why not?

    c. Do you think self-driving cars will become more popular in the future? Do you think they will eventually replace all cars?

    d. How do you feel about other types of self-driving technology?

        i.   buses?

        ii.   taxis?

        iii.   airplanes?

e. Write a short essay or discuss your answer to agree or disagree with the following statements:

    i.   A future with only self-driving cars will be much safer.

    ii.   Driving a car is an important skill all people should learn.

    iii.   A machine can never make decisions as well as a human.

Time Travel 1: Kill Hitler

The Situation:

An amazing thing has just been developed — a Time Machine that can travel back in time! Unfortunately, the technology is in the very early stages and after using the machine once, it will break and need many months or years to rebuild. You've been chosen to make the first trip back in time. You will do something that will change history forever. Because of your military background and German-language skills, you will be sent to kill Adolf Hitler, the leader of the Nazis and responsible for millions of deaths during WWII. You will be sent back to 1920, while Hitler was just an artist and had yet to damage any lives. You are assigned to kill a man who will become a monster… while he is still innocent!

The Dilemma:

CAN YOU MURDER SOMEONE TO SAVE LIVES AND CHANGE HISTORY?

1. What Would You Do? (Explain your reasoning)

a. Accept the assignment and go back in time to kill Hitler?

b. Go back in time, but instead of killing Hitler, try to convince him to change his future life path?

c. Decline the assignment and suggest someone else for it.

d. Suggest a different time to travel to instead?

e. _____

2. Variables: How would it change the situation if...

a. you are asked to kill Hitler when he's a baby?

b. instead of a military background, your job is a...

   i. German-language teacher?

   ii. German historian?

   iii. doctor?

c. you are Jewish and some of your family was killed in the Holocaust?

d. you are German and have some relation to Hitler, so killing him could erase you or your family!

e. _____

3. Expansion Activities for Discussion and Writing

a. Do you think time travel will ever be possible? Why or why not?

   i. Do you think we will be able to use time travel to fix past mistakes?

   ii. If so, what could some unintended consequences be?

b. Who is one person from your country's history who did evil things? Would you erase them from history if you could? How would that change your country's history?

c. If you could go back in time only once, when and where would you go? What would you do?

d. Read the following expression and write a short essay or discuss whether you agree or disagree:

"Those who do not learn history are doomed to repeat it."—George Santayana, Philosopher

   i. What does this quote mean?

   ii. Do you agree or disagree with this statement? Why?

Technology & Future/Politics · # *Time Travel 2: Save JFK*

The Situation:

An amazing thing has just been developed — a Time Machine that can travel back in time! Unfortunately, the technology is in the very early stages and after using the machine once, it will break and need many months or years to rebuild. You've been chosen to make the first trip back in time. You will do something that will change history forever. Because of your military background, you will be sent to save John F. Kennedy, the 35th President of the United States. He was considered to be one of the best presidents in history, but was killed early in his Presidency. JFK, as he is commonly known, was assassinated on November 22, 1963 by a gunman in Dallas.

You want to save JFK, but are worried about the effects of changing history. If you say no, there is another person waiting and excited about taking the assignment!

The Dilemma:

ARE YOU WILLING TO CHANGE HISTORY?

1. What Would You Do? (Explain your reasoning)

a. accept the assignment and go back in time to save JFK?

b. go back in time, but instead of saving JFK, allow his death to happen to allow history to continue?

c. decline the assignment and suggest someone else for it.

d. suggest a different time to travel to instead?

e. _____

2. Variables: How would it change the situation if...

a. you are asked to kill the person or persons who will shoot JFK?

b. instead of a military background, your job is...

    i. English-language teacher?

    ii. American historian?

    iii. doctor?

c. you are related to JFK, so killing him could cause changes for you or your family!

d. _____

3. Expansion Activities for Discussion and Writing:

a. Do you think time travel could ever be possible, to the past, future, or both? Why or why not?

    i. Do you think we may be able to prevent past tragedies?

    ii. If so, what would the consequences be?

b. What do you know about JFK? How do you think saving his life might have changed history?

c. Think of a person in your country's history with a heroic reputation who died young. How would saving them or helping them live longer make a difference in your country's history?

d. If you could go back in time only once, when and where would you go? What would you do?

e. Read the following famous quote from JFK and **write a short essay or discuss** whether you agree or disagree:

"Ask not what your country can do for you, ask what you can do for your country."

    i. What does this quote mean?

    ii. Do you agree or disagree with this statement? Why?

Ethics
Explicit

· # *The Casting Couch*[3]

The Situation:

You're walking on the street one day when you get spotted on the street by a talent agent. You are invited to audition for a big new movie! They are looking for an unknown actor and think you could be perfect for the part! But when you go to the audition, there is only one person there, the producer. After hearing you read some lines from the script, the producer tells you that you will get the part, but only if you're willing to start dating them!

The Dilemma:

WHAT ARE YOU WILLING TO DO FOR FAME AND SUCCESS?

---

3 The term casting couch refers to the practice of casting directors or producers asking for sexual favors from actresses in order to get roles in movies.

1. What Would You Do? (Explain your reasoning)

a. Accept the proposition to get the part?

b. Try to avoid the proposition but still try to get the part?

c. Reject the proposition and the part?

d. _____

2. Variables: How would it change the situation if...

a. the producer is...

   i. very young? very old?

   ii. very handsome or beautiful?

   iii. a man? a woman?

b. instead of a movie, the audition is for...

   i. a live play

   ii. a TV show?

   iii. a music group?

   iv. other _____

c. instead of a movie part, you are simply offered one million dollars to spend the night with the producer.

d. _____

3. Expansion Activities for Discussion and Writing:

a. The term "casting couch" refers to the well-documented situation where casting directors or producers ask for sexual favors from actresses in order to get roles in movies. Do you think this will still happen in the future? Why or why not?

b. Do you know of any real-life examples of this? What happened afterwards?

c. Why do you think this situation happens?

   i. Is it more of an issue for women or men? Why do you think so?

   ii. Is it common in your country/city?

d. **Write about or discuss** the following topic(s):

   i. How does the *casting couch* situation happen? Why does it happen?

   ii. How can we change this situation in the future?

Ethics
Explicit

· *Inappropriate Proposal*

The Situation

You are a very beautiful eighteen-year-old woman. Unfortunately, your family is poor and you don't have much money. You are smart and have been given a partial scholarship to one of the best colleges in the world, but you won't be able to afford it! Your kind and loyal boyfriend is currently working hard, but his financial support won't be even close to enough!

One night, while out at a restaurant with some of your friends, who are paying for your meal as a way of apologizing for your bad luck, a strange old man of at least 70 approaches you. He asks to speak to you privately. Although you are scared, his clothes look extremely expensive and his manner is polite, so you agree.

He says, "My dear, you are the most beautiful creature on Earth, second only to my deceased wife! If you would spend one night with an old man near the end of his long life, I will give you one million dollars."

The Dilemma

CAN YOU SPEND A NIGHT ALONE WITH HIM FOR $ONE MILLION?

1. What Would You Do? (Explain your reasoning)

  a. Accept the proposal and stay with the old man?

  b. Accept the proposal but tell the old man you refuse to do anything sexual?

  c. Go talk to your friends and follow their advice?

  d. Call your boyfriend and follow his advice?

  e. Reject the proposal?

  f. _____

2. Variables: How would it change the situation if...

  a. you are an 18-year-old man and the proposal is from a 70-year-old woman?

  b. you are a woman and the proposal is from an old woman?

  c. you are a man and the proposal is from a man?

  d. your friends (or boyfriend/girlfriend)

   i. think you should accept the proposal?

   ii. think you shouldn't accept the proposal?

  e. _____?

3. Expansion Activities for Discussion and Writing

  a. Do you know of any situations where a much younger person married someone older for money? Would you ever be willing to do this?

  b. If you were rich, would you be willing to be in a relationship with someone much younger who just wants your money?

  c. Which do you think is more common, and why?

   i. A rich older man marrying a younger woman?

   ii. A rich older man marrying a younger man?

  d. **Write a short essay or discuss** your answer to agree or disagree with the following statements:

   i. Money can't buy happiness.

   ii. Money can't buy you love.

   iii. Everyone needs money; that's why they call it money.

Ethics · *Jump on the Grenade*

The Situation:

You're on a military mission with ten other men and women in your unit. You have all worked together and become close over the past year. As you are exploring an old building together the unthinkable happens — a hand grenade is suddenly thrown into the room and the only door is slammed shut!

You all look around quickly with desperation, but there are no windows and no other doors in the small room. The grenade will explode and kill everyone in seconds, unless someone does a very brave thing! If you jump on the grenade, you will die but you will save everyone else.

The Dilemma:

CAN YOU GIVE YOUR LIFE TO SAVE OTHERS?

1. What Would You Do? (Explain your reasoning)

a. Jump on the grenade and give up your life to save everyone?

b. Quickly try to persuade someone else to jump on the grenade?

c. Do nothing and accept your fate!

d. _____?

2. Variables: How would it change the situation if...

a. you're the only member of the unit with a family (husband/wife and children).?

b. you're the only member of the unit without a family?

c. you're the only female member of the unit?

d. there is one female member of the unit?

e. you also have a captured soldier of the other side with you?

f. _____

3. Expansion Activities for Discussion and Writing:

a. If you were in this situation, could you sacrifice your life to save others? Why or why not?

b. Can you think of a similar situation in a TV show or movie? If so, what did the characters do?

c. **Write about or discuss** your response to the following questions:

    i. Many countries, such as Korea, Denmark, and Taiwan, require all citizens, or all male citizens, to serve in the army for at least a short period. Is compulsory military service a good idea?

    ii. Is the death of innocent civilians in war, or collateral damage, sometimes unavoidable or even completely unacceptable?

    iii. Should women be on the front lines in war?

    iv. Is serving in the military a noble thing?

Language · *Global English*

The Situation:

You are on a special global council making a decision that will affect the entire world — whether to make English the official global language. This new global law would make English the official language of the world and taught in all schools all over the world. The goal is to make the world truly speak the same language!

On a council representing countries from all over the world, the vote is tied. You are the last vote and your choice will change how language is used and taught in the entire world!

The Dilemma:

WOULD THE WORLD BE A BETTER PLACE IF WE ALL SPOKE ONE LANGUAGE?

1. What Would You Do? (Explain your reasoning)

    a. Vote for the law to make English the world's global language?

    b. Vote against the law and prevent English replacing other languages?

    c. Ask someone else's opinion and vote their suggestion?

    d. Refuse to vote?

    e. _____

2. Variables: How would it change the situation if...

    a. the entire council is voting unanimously…

        i. to support Global English?

        ii. against Global English?

    b. you are an English teacher and you will have fewer job opportunities if the law is passed?

    c. instead of English, a different language is being voted on to become the world's global language?

        i. Chinese?

        ii. Arabic?

        iii. Other _____

    d. the new law would also make it illegal to teach or study any other languages?

    e. _____

3. Expansion Activities for Discussion and Writing:

    a. Do you think a situation like this could ever be possible? Why or why not?

    b. Do you think more or less people in the world will speak English in the future?

        i. What other languages do you think will become more popular?

        ii. What languages will become less popular?

    c. Why is it important to study other languages?

    d. **Debate:** Is a global language a good idea? With a partner or in groups, debate both sides of this argument?

    e. **Write a short essay or discuss** your answer to one of the following statements:

        i. Language is a necessary part of culture.

        ii. Speaking different languages divides people; speaking the same language would bring us closer.

Ethics   · *Strangers on a Train*

The Situation:

You're riding alone on a train. Suddenly, a serious, scary-looking man in a black suit sits next to you. He shows you a picture of a man who he says is sitting in the next train car. Then he places a gun in your lap. He lists the names some of the people closest to you (for example, your parents, brother/sister, or children) and tells you they will all die if you don't shoot this man in the picture! You have 10 minutes to decide…

The Dilemma:

WOULD YOU MURDER A STRANGER TO SAVE YOUR FAMILY?

1. What Would You Do? (Explain your reasoning)

a. Shoot and kill the innocent stranger?

b. Refuse to use the gun?

c. Shoot the man in the black suit?

d. _____?

2. Variables: How would it change the situation if…

a. you have to shoot a/an _____ instead?

   i. woman

   ii. child

   iii. old man or woman

   iv. animal (like a dog or cat)

b. you were offered one million dollars to shoot the stranger?

c. the stranger you are told to shoot is a…

   i. convicted murderer

   ii. convicted rapist

   iii. dangerous criminal who wasn't convicted?

d. _____

3. Expansion Activities for Discussion and Writing

a. Do you think this situation could ever be possible? Why or why not?

b. Can you think of a similar situation in a TV show or movie? If so, what did the characters do?

c. **Write about or discuss** what you think about…

   i. the death penalty for serious criminals.

   ii. vigilante justice, killing a suspected criminal before he's been convicted?

   iii. is assassination ever justified?

Ethics · *Terror Attack*

The Situation:

You're taking a peaceful nap on an airplane when you suddenly awaken to a loud noise — a single, male terrorist of average size is standing in the aisle, holding a gun, and yelling! You are sitting alone in the very back row. You were sleeping under a blanket, and he must not have seen you. In fact, the terrorist is standing right in front of your row, with his back turned. You, only you, seem to have missed the terrorist's attention.

The Dilemma:

WOULD YOU TRY TO STOP THE TERRORIST?

1. What Would You Do? (Explain your reasoning)

a. Try to jump the terrorist from behind?

b. Try to signal someone else for help?

c. Try to talk to the terrorist?

d. Pretend to go back to sleep and hope you keep being ignored?

e. Do nothing but keep watching?

f. _____

2. Variables: How would it change the situation if...

a. the terrorist is...

    i. much bigger than you?

    ii. much smaller than you?

    iii. a woman?

    iv. speaks the same foreign language as you?

    v. an old friend you recognize?

b. instead of a plane you are...

    i. on a bus or train?

    ii. at school?

    iii. in a movie theater?

    iv. in a café?

c. You are a(n)...

    i. air marshal

    ii. police officer

    iii. karate instructor

    iv. hostage negotiator

d. _____

3. Expansion Activities for Discussion and Writing:

a. Do you think this situation could ever be possible? Why or why not

b. Do you know of any similar situations in your country? What happened?

c. Do you ever worry about terrorist attacks in public places?

      i.   Which places worry you most?

      ii.   Do you do anything to prepare?

d. Read the following expression and **write a short essay or discuss** if you agree or disagree:

"The only way to stop a bad guy with a gun is with a good guy with a gun." —Wayne LaPierre, Former CEO, the National Rifle Association (NRA)

Ethics & History

· The Titanic: Women and Children First

The Situation:

It's 1918, you are a man, and you are on the beautiful ship the *Titanic* which is enjoying its maiden voyage from England to New York — until the ship hits an iceberg and starts sinking. Unfortunately, the ship is not prepared and there aren't enough lifeboats, so many people will die. The captain announces that women and children will be put on the lifeboats first, leaving some of the men to die…including you!

The Dilemma:

CAN YOU ACCEPT DYING TO PROTECT OTHERS?

1. What Would You Do? (Explain your reasoning)

   a. Accept that you will die so the women and children can live?

   b. Talk to the captain about why you are special and should be on a lifeboat?

   c. Talk to the captain about how his decision is discrimination and try to come up with another plan?

   d. Try to sneak on a lifeboat?

   e. _____

2. Variables: How would it change the situation if...

   a. you are over 70 years old?

   b. you are 18 years old?

   c. you are a woman?

   d. you are the captain?

   e. most of the women on the ship are old and the men are young?

   f. _____

3. Expansion Activities for Discussion and Writing:

   a. Do you think this kind of tragic situation could ever be possible again? Why or why not?

   b. Why do you think women and children were given preference over (some) men on the lifeboats?

   c. In addition to women and children, more rich than poor passengers survived the sinking. Why do you think this is?

   d. This is an example of a life-and-death situation. How would you act in this situation? Do you think you could be brave?

   e. **Write about or discuss the following topic(s):** On Only 705 out of 2,208 passengers and crew survived the sinking of the *Titanic*.[4]

      i. How would you have chosen who got into the lifeboats first?

      ii. Who should make this decision?

---

4 Andrew Wilson. "Curse of the Titanic: What Happened to Those Who Survived?" *The Independent*. October 28, 2011. https://www.independent.co.uk/arts-entertainment/books/features/curse-of-the-titanic-what-happened-to-those-who-survived-6252311.html.

Politics   · *Open Borders*

The Situation:

You are at a global meeting representing your country on the issue of *open borders*. Open borders, or 'free movement' means eliminating visas between countries for travel, work, or living. Borders and countries remain, but anyone is free to work or live where they choose!

The person presenting the supporting opinion on this issue claims it is unfair that some are lucky or unlucky depending on where they are born and that free movement will be good for the world economy.

The person against is concerned that many countries will lose their unique culture and that too many people from poor countries will move to rich ones.

The world's vote is now tied, and your vote will decide the future of the world's borders!

The Dilemma:

DO YOU VOTE FOR OR AGAINST OPEN BORDERS?

1. What Would You Do? (Explain your reasoning)

a. Vote for open borders?

b. Vote against open borders?

c. _____

2. Variables: How would it change the situation if…

a. Your country is very rich?

b. Your country is very poor?

c. Each country can choose to make its borders open or closed?

   i.   What would you choose for your country?

d. You have 30 minutes to decide and can ask one person to help decide for you?

   i.   Who would you ask?

e. Global criminal records will be kept and anyone with a record won't be allowed free movement?

   i.   OR criminal records won't be shared between countries?

f. _____

3. Expansion Activities for Discussion and Writing:

a. Have you ever gotten a visa for travel or work? If so, was the process easy or difficult?

b. Have you or someone that you know ever had trouble traveling or staying in a country? If so, what happened?

c. **Research and write:** Research the 'open borders' or 'free movement' issue.

   i.   Use at least one source to argue for or against this issue.

d. Write about or discuss the following topic(s):

   i.   Major problems in any country should be helped by all.

   ii.   It's important to solve all the problems of our own countries before helping others.

   iii.   We should think of all people as one race and make it easier to live and work together.

   iv.   Keeping strong borders between countries is necessary.

Ethics · *Stealing to Save*

The Situation:

One of the cleaning staff at your office is having family troubles. His family has three kids and many hospital bills. His wife has a disability and cannot work, and his youngest child is sick with a deadly illness. He is often upset at work, even crying. He complains to you, and others, privately that his youngest child may die without expensive medical treatment.

One night, the office is robbed and a lot of money and valuable things are taken. A few days later, the cleaning staff member seems much happier. You are pretty sure he was involved. You go to ask him and he gets very upset. Privately, he offers you a good amount of money to keep quiet. He begs you to not turn him in for the sake of his family!

The Dilemma:

IS IT EVER OK TO STEAL, IF IT'S TO HELP PEOPLE?

1. What Would You Do? (Explain your reasoning)

a. Take the money and say nothing?

b. Try to convince the cleaning staff member to turn himself in?

c. Talk to your boss or police and tell them the truth about the robbery?

d. _____

2. Variables: How would it change the situation if...

a. The cleaning staff is...

   i. very young or old?

   ii. male or female?

   iii. an undocumented foreigner from another country?

b. Instead of a sick child, the cleaning staff needs money for a sick...

   i. parent/grandparent?

   ii. spouse?

   iii. dog?

c. The cleaning staff member offers you all the money to stay quiet if you don't turn him in?

d. _____

3. Expansion Activities for Discussion and Writing:

a. Have you or anyone you know ever stolen something to help someone?

b. Do you think it's ever ok to steal? If yes, what kind of situation is acceptable?

c. In some countries, stealing is strictly punished. For example, thieves may have their hands cut off!

   i. What do you think is the appropriate punishment for stealing?

   ii. How much does the value of what is stolen affect the crime?

d. Does taking something with little value (such as eating single grapes at the supermarket) count as stealing?

e. Does stealing a higher value item (such as a car) deserve a stricter punishment than something less valuable (like a bag or phone)?

f. **Discuss or write** a short response to one of the following statements:

   i. Any parent would be willing to steal to save their child.

   ii. The traditional folk hero Robin Hood was personified by the following statement: *"Steal from the rich, give to the poor."*
   - Do you agree or disagree with his statement? Why?

Ethics   · *The Trolley Problem*

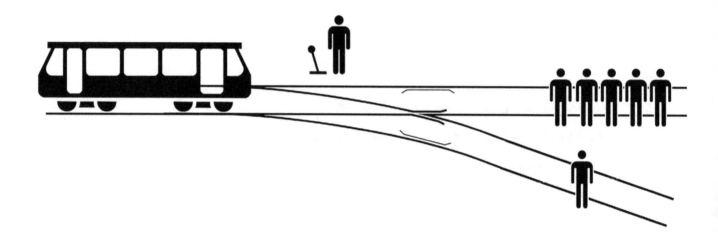

The Situation:

The trolley problem is a famous thought experiment designed to make people think about ethics. Philippa Foot proposed this form of the problem in 1967.

There is a runaway trolley barreling down the railway tracks. Ahead on the tracks, there are five people tied up and unable to move. The trolley is headed straight for them. You are standing some distance off in the train yard, next to a lever. If you pull this lever, the trolley will switch to a different set of tracks. However, you notice that there is one person tied up on the side track. There is no way to stop the train or untie the people. Your only choice is whether to pull the lever or not!

The Dilemma:

IS IT BETTER TO KILL ONE PERSON IN ORDER TO SAVE THE LIVES OF MANY?

1. What Would You Do? (Explain your reasoning)

a. Do nothing, and let the trolley kill the five people on the main track.

b. Pull the lever, diverting the trolley onto the side track where it will kill one person.

c. _____

2. Variables: How would it change the situation if…

a. the five people are all…

    i.   over 60 years old?

    ii.   babies?

    iii.   under 10 years old?

    iv.   women

    v.   men

b. the one person is…

    i.   over 60 years old?

    ii.   under 10 years old

    iii.   a baby

    iv.   a woman

    v.   a man

c. _____

3. Expansion Activities for Discussion and Writing:

a. Can you think of a real situation where someone might have to make a decision about whether to save or abandon a group of people?

    i.   What would you do in this realistic situation?

b. Can you think of a similar dilemma in a book or a TV show or movie? What did the character decide? Who was saved?

c. **Design your own ethical thought experiment:** There must be two or more choices, all resulting in harmful effects.

    i.   What is the situation?

    ii.   What would you do in this situation?

    iii.   Ask your friends or family what they would do?

d. **Research and write:** There are many variations of 'The Trolley Problem' where one or more people must be sacrificed to save others. For example, the *Organ Donor Problem*: Would you kill one person to take their organs to save five?

    i.   Research another variation of 'The Trolley Problem'
- What is the sacrifice?
- What would you do in this situation?

    ii.   Or create your own ethical dilemma problem!
- What is the sacrifice?
- What would you do in this situation?

e. **Write about or discuss t**he following quote: "The needs of the many outweigh the needs of the few." — Charles Dickens, *A Tale of Two Cities*

    i.   What does this quote mean? Do you agree or disagree?

SUPPLEMENT 1:

Essay Writing

- Write an essay related to the dilemma from the topic
- Write 3-5 paragraphs (about 200 words)

TOPIC: ....

DILEMMA: ....

SUPPLEMENT 2:

Dilemma Debates

Choose two solutions for the dilemma. Write some pros for each solution.

You can also adapt the dilemma or choose a variable to make a more exciting debate!

TOPIC: _____

DILEMMA: _____

SOLUTION 1	SOLUTION 2

Which answer do you agree with most? Why?

_____

_____

_____

_____

_____

_____

Which answer do you disagree with most? Why?

_____

_____

_____

_____

SUPPLEMENT 4:

Experiment

Design an experiment to test the dilemma presented in the book! For your experiment, you should do one the following:

- Create a real situation and test friends'/family/strangers' reactions

- Write an interview question describing a dilemma and ask it

- Your own creative idea!

DILEMMA:

DESCRIBE THE EXPERIMENT (WHAT ARE YOU GOING TO DO?)

HYPOTHESIS (WHAT DO YOU EXPECT TO HAPPEN?)

RESULTS (TRY TO GET THREE OR MORE RESULTS)

CONCLUSION (WERE THE RESULTS WHAT YOU EXPECTED? WHY OR WHY NOT?)

SUPPLEMENT 5:

Create a Story

Choose one of the following and write~1 page (less than 200 words)

- **Summarize** the dilemma in your own words.

- **Rewrite** the dilemma into a fictional story

DILEMMA:

SUPPLEMENTS 6:

Drama

Make a Live Drama Scene

In a group, adapt your dilemma situation into a live drama scene!

Your scene should have the following three elements:

(some examples are listed below)

SETTING:	CHARACTERS:	SITUATION:
Where is the scene taking place?	How many characters are in your scene? Who are they?	What is the action of the scene?
At school	Friends	Arguing/Fighting
At a store	Family	Romance
In a dream	Strangers	Having dinner

Write the plan for your project below:

ORIGINAL DILEMMA/SITUATION: _____

_____

_____

_____

_____

PLAN: WRITE OUT THE PLAN FOR YOUR SCENE!

SETTING:	CHARACTERS:	SITUATION:

SCRIPT:

(Write out the full dialogue on another sheet of paper)

SUPPLEMENTS 7:

Make a Movie

In a group, adapt your dilemma situation into a short film! You can choose one of these three approaches:

TRAILER:	DILEMMA:	FULL DRAMA/MOVIE:
Make a short preview of the dilemma!	Turn the situation into a short one scene Film.	Turn the dilemma into a longer, five-to-ten-minute story.

Write the notes for your project below:

MOVIE TITLE: _____

_____

_____

_____

_____

TRAILER, IMPORTANT SCENE, OR FULL MOVIE? _____

_____

_____

_____

_____

NOTES: (SUMMARIZE YOUR STORY BEFORE YOU MAKE IT!)

SCRIPT:

(Write out the full dialogue on another sheet of paper)

SUPPLEMENTS 8:

Create Your Own Dilemma

Create your own interesting dilemma! Follow the steps below! Add a picture/drawing if you can!

TITLE:

Add drawing/picture here!

MOVIE TITLE:

THE SITUATION

(Describe in a short paragraph)

THE DILEMMA

(In one sentence, describe the dilemma)

WHAT WOULD YOU DO?

(Write 3 or more options)

VARIABLES: HOW WOULD IT CHANGE THE SITUATION IF...

(Write 3 or more Variables)

EXPANSION ACTIVITIES FOR DISCUSSION AND WRITING

(Write 2 or more Extra Questions related to your dilemma)

SUPPLEMENT 9-1:

Simple Dilemma Cards

Use the cards below for discussion, writing, or other activities.

SIMPLE DILEMMA CONVERSATION CARDS

1. Would you keep a new pet if your sibling was allergic to it?	10. Would you be a teacher's pet to get better grades?	19. Would you still study languages if you could wear a device that could translate any language instantly?
2. Would you eat a dinner at a friend's house if you hated the cooking?	11. Would you be willing to take three hours of cram school after school to prepare for college?	20. What would you wish for if you had three wishes?
3. Would you tell your friend who has a hygiene problem?	12. Would you give a homeless person your change?	21. Would you leave if there was a ghost in your bedroom?
4. Would you kill a spider in your house or try to put it outside?	13. Would you try to help if you saw a dog alone in a hot car?	22. What would you do if your pet could talk?
5. Would you be willing to live with someone with a scary pet (like a spider or snake?)	14. Would you return a lost wallet you found on the street filled with money?	23. Would you be willing to fight a dragon if you had a magic wand?

6. Would you tell a friend who's always serious to smile more?	15. Would you be willing to live on Mars?	24. Would you run away or fight if a ninja was hired to kill you?
7. Would you tell the truth if you're late to class for no good reason?	16. What one type of information would you like to learn instantly right now?	25. Would you become a superhero if you had superpowers? (flying, super strength, vision, etc..)
8. Would you tell the teacher if you saw someone cheating on an important test?	17. Would you wear your phone as contacts on your eyes?	26. Who or what would you save first if a volcano was about to destroy your house?
9. Would you rather have uniforms or no uniforms at school?	18. Would you approach or run away if you saw a space alien?	27. What would you do if a zombie bit you?

SUPPLEMENT 9-2:

Medium Dilemma Cards

Use the cards below for discussion, writing, or other activities.

MEDIUM DILEMMA CONVERSATION CARDS

1. What would you do if your friend had a drug problem?	10. Would you hug a stranger with a sign that said Free Hugs?	19. Where would you go if you could be in any place in the world at this second?
2. What would you do if someone you know likes to touch you too much?	11. Would you take your laptop or valuables with you to the restroom at a café?	20. Would you be willing to change your gender? (for one day/1 year)
3. What would you do if your friend is always late?	12. What would you do if your neighbor is always making loud sounds late?	21. What would you do if you had the choice to be able to live forever?
4. Would you ever try online dating? What if the person was less attractive in person than in the pictures online?	13. What would you do if you and your roommate disagree about taking off shoes inside your apartment?	22. What would you do if you could read any person's mind?
5. What would you do if you and your partner disagree about PDA (Public Display of Affection)?	14. What would you do if really had to go to the bathroom and only the opposite-gender toilet was open?	23. Would you do if you were the leader of a country?

6. What would you do if your 12-old child wants to start dating and asks your advice?	15. What would you do if a young child was being really loud and annoying in public (like at a nice restaurant)?	24. What would you do if you won $50 million in the lottery?
7. What would you do if you found out someone you were dating was transgender?	16. Would you want to have a clone of yourself?	25. What would you do if you saw your favorite celebrity in person?
8. What would you do if someone you know always likes to get too close when talking?	17. Would you be willing to have a robot as a romantic partner?	26. What would you do if your friends wanted you to go hunting?
9. Would you tip if the service at a restaurant was really bad?	18. Would you like to be able to get rid of painful memories?	27. Would you be willing to give a job to an illegal alien?

SUPPLEMENT 9-3:

Advanced Dilemma Cards

Use the cards below for discussion, writing, or other activities.

ADVANCED DILEMMA CONVERSATION CARDS

1. What would you do if your child likes to listen to music with inappropriate lyrics? (violence, sexism, racism, etc..)	10. What would you do if you and your partner have different religious beliefs but you love them very much?	19. What would you do if a strange old person offered you $1 million to spend the night with them?
2. What would you do to discipline your child if they won't listen to you?	11. What would you do if people at your café complain about no *gender-neutral* restroom?	20. What would you do if you could sacrifice your life to save many others?
3. How would you stop or limit your child's smartphone use?	12. What would you do if you had to lie about your experience to get a great job?	21. What would you do if you could make English the only language spoken in the world?
4. What would you do if you and your partner disagree about where to have your baby sleep (in the same or a different room)?	13. What would you do if the world is too overpopulated and you must choose going to Mars or death?	22. What would you do if someone threatened to hurt your family if you don't do a crime (rob a bank, murder, etc.)?
5. What would you do if your partner cheated on you but asked for forgiveness?	14. What would you do if a young child was being really loud and annoying in public (like at a nice restaurant)?	23. What would you do if you saw a terrorist about to attack sitting next to you on a train or airplane?

6. What would you do if your friends who are always dating are fighting and never get along?	15. What would you do if your new work partner was a robot?	24. What would you do if were on a sinking ship and you could only choose 10 out of 100 people to save?
7. What would you do if you love your partner much more than they love you?	16. What would you do if your new smart car was driving itself and hit a person?	25. What would you had to choose to help three old people in danger or one baby?
8. What would you do if your partner wanted to be intimate in a public area (like an airplane restroom)?	17. What would you do if you could go back and time and stop a dangerous or evil person (like Hitler)?	26. What would you do if countries could eliminate visas to allow free travel and work between countries?
9. What would you do if your partner never wants to say *I love you*?	18. What would you do if you could go back and time and save any person's life?	27. What would you do if your child was sick and you needed to steal to save them?

SUPPLEMENTS 10:

What Would They Do?

- Choose a topic and read the situation, dilemma, and "what would you do" choices as a class and as groups.

- Each student writes the situation, their answer, and why in the box below.

- Afterwards either in groups or as a full class have Ss go one-by-one and see if their partners can guess their answer. Give one point to any person/group that can guess What Would They Do correctly!

You can use the **Dilemma Choice Cards** on the next page to have Ss put down their guesses! You can play anywhere from 1-5 rounds depending on time and group sizes!

WHAT THEY DO ANSWER SHEET: NAME:

Situation/Dilemma	What Would You Do Answer (circle one)	Why?
	A / B / C / D / E / F	
	A / B / C / D / E / F	
	A / B / C / D / E / F	
	A / B / C / D / E / F	
	A / B / C / D / E / F	

"What Would They Do" Dilemma Choice Cards

A	B	C
D	E	F

A	B	C
D	E	F

SUPPLEMENT 10:

Create Your Own Answer!

- Each student/group gets the three slips below.

- Choose a topic and read the situation and dilemma as a class or as groups.

- Each student/group writes the situation, their own original answer, and why in the box on the next page.

- Afterwards either in groups or as a full class read all of the answers and as a class vote on which is the best one. The student/group with the best answer gets a point!

- You can play anywhere from 1-3 rounds depending on time and group sizes!

SITUATION 1

What Would You Do and Why?

SITUATION 2

What Would You Do and Why?

SITUATION 3

What Would You Do and Why?

SUPPLEMENTS 10:

No-Prep Dilemma Games

Defend Your Choice!

- Read a situation, dilemma, and choices.

- Give each student one of the Dilemma Choice Cards matching one of the choices from the situation.

- Give each student ~1 minute to defend this choice, either in groups or as a whole class.

Most Popular!

- Read a situation, dilemma, and choices.

- Have students stand up or raise their hand at their choice.

- Write the most popular choice on the board.

- The Students who made this choice should defend it to the rest of the class.

Variation:

- Students should try and guess which option is most popular.

- You can also use the **Dilemma Choice Cards** to help students vote.

Draw It!

- The teacher chooses three situations and writes them on the board. Each student/group draws a picture of one of the situations.

- Afterwards as a whole class/in groups students try to match the picture and situation and vote which is best!

About the Author

Taylor has two great passions: writing and teaching. He has spent over 10 years as an educator of ESL students across different universities and private schools in Japan and America, and currently teaches English at ELS Portland. He is also the author of *Stories Without End*.

The dilemma of choosing waking up early for writing versus more sleep helped lead directly to this book! Another important dilemma is when your son asks to add one of his pictures to your book!

OTHER BOOKS BY ALPHABET PUBLISHING

Stories Without End: 24 open-ended stories to engage students with reading, discussion, and creative writing
Taylor Sapp

These unfinished story-prompts will engage even the most reluctant writer in your class.

60 Positive Activities for Every Classroom
Created by Teresa X. Nguyen. Illustrated by Nathaniel Cayanan

60 illustrated prompts for teenagers and young adults to discuss and write about while reflecting on the bright side of life.

60 Positive Activities for Kids
Created by Teresa X. Nguyen. Illustrated by Tyler Hoang

These creative discussion or writing prompts are designed to get kids talking and creating while building positivity.

Successful Group Work: 13 Activities to Teach Teamwork Skills
Patrice Palmer

Teach the teamwork skills your students need to do group projects in the classroom and in the workplace.

50 Activities for the First Day of School
Walton Burns

Never stress about the first day of class again!

Classroom Community Builders: *Activities for the First Day & Beyond*
Walton Burns

Break the ice, build rapport, and teach content with these practical and engaging activities that make efficient use of every minute of class time.

Alphabet Publishing is a small, independent publishing company that specializes in creative resources for teachers in the area of English Language Arts and English as a Second or Other Language. We help stock the teacher toolkit with practical, useful, and innovative materials.

Sign up for our mailing list at alphabetpublishingbooks.com for resources, discounts, and giveaways you won't find anywhere else.

CPSIA information can be obtained
at www.ICGtesting.com
Printed in the USA
LVHW060549160819
627878LV00005B/22/P